GOD'S TRUTH

AS REVEALED BY SAM SINGLETON, ATHEIST EVANGELIST

• Patriarchs and Penises • If the Ocean was Whiskey (and God was a Duck) • Revival •
• Cats, Sheep and Goats: the Taxonomy of Atheists, Believers and Preachers •
• and more •

ROGER SCOTT JACKSON

This book is sold by weight, not by volume.

Cover photo by Cari Park
Back cover photo by Daylon Walton
Book design by Troy Malibu

This edition includes works previously published by Flag Knob Publishers,
copyright Sam Singleton, Atheist Evangelist/Roger Scott Jackson:
Harmony (1997)
Postcards from Paul (1999)
Patriarchs and Penises (2007)
Atheists at Prayer (2008)
Gimme an A (2008)
If the Ocean was Whiskey and God was a Duck (2009)
Why Atheists Always Lose When Debating the Existence of God (2009)
Brother Sam's Rules of Engagement (2009)
One of the Lucky Ones (2009)
Why Brother Sam is not Brother John (2010)
Revival (2011)
Cats, Sheep and Goats:
the Taxonomy of Atheists, Believers and Preachers (2012)

ISBN 978-0-692-41428-6

Secular Media Group LLC

in association with
Flag Knob Publishers
a Division of
Dogberry, Bottom and Sly LLC

Printed in the U.S.A.

Brewing
Baking
Distilling
Farming
Frying
Roasting
Fermentation
Smoking
Domesticating the Dog

This book is dedicated to those responsible
for these and the many other discoveries
and innovations that add joy to my life.
And Cari, of course.

Introduction

I've known Sam Singleton, Atheist Evangelist since his conception in 2007. He wrote his first show, *Patriarchs and Penises* that year. Since then there have been many tours and countless shows, all over the country, for audiences large and small. To the fans, with whom he has an especially close bond, he's just Brother Sam. People holler "goddamn" (his personal catch prase) in greeting at conferences and at shows, in hotels and in pubs. On stage he's a commanding figure. Off stage he's warm and personable.

I have been beside him at every point of his journey, both literally and figuratively. As his tour manager, stage hand, editor, director, driver, wardrobe supervisor, food taster, confidante and wife, I've seen every aspect of Brother Sam's life.

During these years I have received a religious education from the Atheist Evangelist himself. Brother Sam KNOWS this shit. It is in his blood, even though his mind has long since outgrown the fable. Furthermore, he has made a concerted study of the world's theologies.

I, a lifelong atheist, had never been exposed to religion's doctrines, dogmas and delusions. I feel fortunate to have been spared; happy to be free of religion, at least in my personal life.

But, personal choices and preferences only protect me so far in a society where upwards of eighty percent of Americans believe that their god created them and made the rules. They insist that 'God's' rules apply to me, and all the world, too.

This is why Brother Sam's message is important. He is in a unique position to present the atheist to the believer, and vice-versa. He combines scholarship, humor, original thinking and personal recollection in his stories to reach audiences from many angles.

Brother Sam has put himself in some personal danger, as any truth-teller and blasphemer will who publicly questions-nay, ridicules-the belief in supernatural beings common to the Christian majority in the USA. There have been threats and curses; shows have been interrupted and shut down; venues have been denied.

For each negative word or action, there are hundreds of gratifying responses to the word of Sam Singleton, Atheist Evangelist. After every performance a crowd of grateful fans offer their heartfelt gratitude to the man whose words have expressed the thoughts and feelings they have struggled with for years. They recognize a fellow traveler with the ability to explain the complex and often conflicting emotions of the religiously oppressed in illuminating language and a folksy manner.

Sam Singleton, Atheist Evangelist fills the niche previously occupied by Mark Twain and Robert G. Ingersoll. I am proud to play a supporting role in presenting Brother Sam and the "GOD'S TRUTH" to you.

Cari Park

Foreword

castigat ridendo mores

Sam Singleton Atheist Evangelist. That's evangelist in the ironic sense. It's a shibboleth, a sort of password. If your sense of irony is not up to "atheist evangelist," no need to bother with the rest.

Patriarchs and Penises, If the Ocean was Whiskey and God was a Duck, Revival, and *Cats, Sheep and Goats: the Taxonomy of Atheists, Believers and Preachers* were written over many years, and performed as individual shows. Together they comprise a single story, which asks (and answers) the question: what would one reared to be a snake-handling Pentecostal preacher have to say if he grew up to be an atheist?

Brother Sam's self-ordained mission is to illuminate and challenge bad beliefs that underlie bad behavior. To commiserate with others in the nonbelieving minority. To offer a bit of encouragement. Maybe raise an occasional chuckle.

Is it mere mockery? Is that all that Brother

Sam's work amounts to? There is nothing "mere" about mockery in the face of immense political and cultural might. One grabs whatever equalizer falls to hand. No conceit is so grandiose that mockery cannot reduce it to a manageable size. Mockery is the blunt instrument with which superstition is rendered insensible; satire is the scalpel with which is performed its vivisection. Goddamn.

RSJ

castigat ridendo mores
one corrects morals by laughing at them

Patriarchs and Penises™
A Comedy in Two Acts

Act I

Goddamn. I always figure that there are three kinds of people that come out to the show: atheists like Brother Sam, agnostics like, well, y'all aren't like anything, and the ones that say they actually believe in God. Theists. And I'm going to be talking to each group at different times and sometimes all together. So pay attention. And I realize that the godly will have to pedal harder to keep up. Maybe you can sit behind an atheist and get carried along in the slipstream.

I'm gonna spend a little time explaining how silly the Bible is and how its main characters are all curiously preoccupied with penises, their own and other guys', which I suppose is inevitable seeing as how the bible is so *patriarchal*. Not much ink gets spilt on the ladies.

Lucky for you, Brother Sam has gone to the trouble of actually reading the Bible so you don't have to. Just like the clergy. You're welcome. And just so you know, you're not missing much. For one thing, that motherfucker is long. And

it just gets sillier and boringer and more rep-
etitious till, and I hate the spoil the ending, till
you've suffered through oh, twelve hundred pag-
es, before you realize that it was nothing but one
of those juvenile gags in which the punch line is
just the word penis. There's no object, no moral
to the damn thing.

Maybe the writers knew what they were doing, given their intended audience. I think they
just must've figured there was no call to exert
themselves, trying to stuff a bunch of actual content into the bible, when all that was necessary
to get all the lurid little snickers and giggles they
were after was to keep steering the story back to
penises.

And you can't get very far into any explora-
tion of biblical dicks before you come upon the
Patriarchs, the bible's heroes, who all made pe-
nile history in various ways

The word monogamy does not appear in the
bible. Neither does incest. We'll get into all that
here in about an hour, in bible class.

My point is that the very people who model
their morality on the examples of the Patriarchs
and their god, are screwing us while we stand.
And the only way to stop them is to say, right out
loud, "Now there may be ten times more of you
all than there are of us, but that don't mean you
can fuck me without me saying something about
it. I'm hitching up my britches and going home."

I hate to be so blunt, but there it is. The

question isn't whether they've got us outnumbered. They have. It's by how much. In the U.S.A.,
the degree to which majorities feel emboldened
to go up your yoohoo without so much as a by-
your-leave is never less than proportionate to
their numerical superiority. In what passes for
a democracy, numbers are important. Get yourselves under counted and you are guaranteed to
be underrepresented, under heard, under paid-
attention-to. Fucked, like I say. Speedily. Might-
ily. Regularly.

I've seen polls that say nonbelievers account for about eleven percent of the population,
which works out to about thirty-one million of
us, double what it was ten years ago. If atheism were a religion, it'd be expanding at a clip
similar to that of the Moslems here in the U.S.A.
And if you think that sounds good, just remember that it still leaves eighty-nine percent of the
folks in the air traffic control towers, at the trig-
gers of the nuclear arsenal, in the government,
the military, and the police, eighty-nine percent
of your fellow Americans, all claiming that they
have an imaginary friend who tells them what to
do. And the ones with the imaginary friend have
combined their individually indolent brains into
a vast mediocre intelligence. It isn't any smarter,
just more powerful. They form a single primitive organism like one of those giant fungi that
spread all over a pasture and sprout poisonous
little toadstools wherever there's a cow plop.

They've turned it into a culture, a form of governance, *mediocracy*, in which eleven percent of the population, the top eleven percent, need not apply.

Being a minority in the U.S.A. is not all it's cracked up to be. In fact, it will get you hosed every time. Or eighty-nine percent of the time.

Part of our problem is that we're not conspicuous enough. We need to dress up funny one day a year and have big atheist pride parades all over the place. That's what we need to do. Rolling over and playing dead has got us mistaken for actually being dead. Do that shit long enough and one morning you're not playing anymore. And if you end up getting a Christian burial don't say you weren't warned. Even when you're dead they'll still be fucking you. Necrotheism. It's the Christians that are supposed to turn the other cheek. I'll tell you one thing about my Christian kin, my cheeks involuntarily clinch whenever I'm around 'em.

Here I'm gonna talk to the godly. Absent any evidence that your imaginary friend, this god that Abraham invented, exists, you'll have to excuse our skepticism. But it's OK. Nobody's telling you that you can't have imaginary friends. Hell, there are times I wish some of my friends were imaginary. But the thing with imaginary friends is, they are not real. That's the imaginary part. And you might not want to let on when you're out in public. Kind of keep God to yourself so people don't think you're nuts. And you must understand that imaginary friends are intrinsically funny. So when people laugh, they're not necessarily laughing at you. By all means, believe what you want. Just don't expect real adults to trust you to look after anything important. And forget about running for office. Belief in imaginary friends should automatically disqualify you from any position of responsibility. It is irrational.

And you gotta wonder how the hell more than half the people on earth got to believing in the same big imaginary friend, who can't really be big since he's just imaginary. The answer is evangelism. And killing the ones that don't buy in. God and genocide. A match made in heaven.

So now you got these three-point-four billion believers in Abraham's god, all the Moslems and Christians and Jews, and instead of figuring as how that gives them all something in common, they just fuss with one another over who gets to decide for everybody else what their imaginary friend, Abraham's god, is like and what his rules are. And that's a whole nuther deal which we'll get to here shortly.

They may hate each other's guts, but they all seem to agree that you can just ratify God into existence. That if you can get enough people to say it's so, it'll actually become so. And I say horseshit.

What I'm invoking here is the time-honored right of the minority to ridicule the majority.

The sacred standing of the tormented to mock their tormentors. So if you can't abide me spanking holes in God's underpants, I got six words: Brother Sam don't give no refunds.

The godly have been pushing me around my entire life. Excuse the hell out of me if, while they take my lunch money, I crack wise about their superstitions. You play the hand that's dealt you.

And yet the godly say to me, "Brother Sam, who the fuck do you think you are to be sacrilegious-izing other people's traditions and beliefs?"

See? That's one of them offensive questions that the only way to answer is defensively. So I generally tell them about my entire heritage amounting to nothing but a Great Dismal Swamp of godly traditions and beliefs. How I just come-a-one of getting sucked under the scum like the rest of my people. And how I went to a deal of trouble to extricate myself. And anybody thinks I don't get to talk about it, anybody wants to shut me up, should go to hell. If they can find one. And I don't mean Michigan.

Now, you see, that sounds harsh. And I promised my darling wife, Sister Singleton, that I'd ease off the mean-mouthing. But goddammit, this god deal just gets up under my hide and pokes at me until I go to getting cranky.

From when I was a baby in swaddling clothes I was groomed for the ministry. Fortunately, I came to my senses before anybody got hurt.

Along about the time certain parts of me got to fuzzing up, I set out to find a way of getting God to reimburse me for some of the shit I've had to put up with, preferably one that didn't involve rooking the gullible out of their wages. And so here we are.

The Gospel According to Bertrand Russell says religion is based mainly on fear— and it sure was for me. My folks, Brother John Calvin Singleton and Sister Maureen Sedgwick Singleton, were not assholes by nature. I'd hate to think that they set out to turn childhood into some kind of freak-show hell-ride for my sisters and me. But try or not, they did a bang-up job.

That passage from Bertrand Russell, here's the rest of it. "Fear is the parent of cruelty, and therefore it is no wonder if cruelty and religion have gone hand in hand."

John Calvin and Maureen sure didn't have any monopoly on using God to terrorize their children. Parents and teachers and preachers have been hard at that particular aspect of the lord's work ever since the Bible first came out as a full-length work of fiction after being serialized in Playboy.

Deuteronomy 31: *And that their children which have not known any thing may hear and learn to fear the lord your God as long as ye live.* Right through to Hebrews 10, where the Apostle Paul says, *It is a fearful thing to fall into the hands of the living God.* And he ain't shittin', neither. It was pretty goddamned fearful just falling into the hands of his kin.

When I was a child, I preferred to think that somebody was putting my folks up to the religious terrorizing they laid on my sisters and me. The gut wrenching part was accepting that there was no God pulling their strings. That everything they did, they did of their own free will. Out of their own self-interest. They loved God more than they loved us. That was obvious from all the horrifying, dangerous, stuff they were willing to expose us to in order to reap the personal rewards of God's favor. Even a child could see, that like everybody who practices any religion, they were ultimately in it for themselves. The final benefit—personal salvation and all that goes with it—couldn't help but go to them alone. It could be lost, you could backslide and fall from grace and wind up burning in hell, but salvation couldn't be transferred to somebody else, couldn't even be shared. I was pretty sure that if it came down to a choice between God and me, I was screwed. I sure as hell knew better than to put it to the test.

So, on one level, I was jealous of God. And that's ironic, since God's pretty fucking neurotic himself, totally fatal-attraction psycho-stalker jealous, and twisted enough to brag about it. All the time. He never shuts up about how jealous he is.

I, the Lord your God, am a jealous God.

That's from Exodus 20, Crazy God's Crazy Crash Course in Craziness. It's so bad that even when his toadies describe him that's the first word that comes to mind. It's who he is. What did Paul write to his pals in Corinth? *Do we provoke the Lord to jealously?* You better goddamn not.

God refers to himself like it's his given name. Here's the direct quote, and I shit you not, Exodus 34:14. *My name is Jealous.* Now, who's going to argue with that? Tomorrow it might be *My name is Spiteful.* Or *Avaricious.* Or *Puddintame.*

You don't have to be a TV psychologist to see that jealousy comes from feelings of inadequacy and insecurity. Everybody experiences some jealousy. But most grown-ups don't— like the kindergarten teachers say: act out. Even little children know better than to act out. God acts out like a motherfucker. When he's displeased with one of his creations, he has him a big old shit fit and just kills everybody as if they mean no more— less to him, than an ant farm does to a little Jeffrey Dahmer. That's what the bible adds up to: earth is a murderous god's ant farm. He's already filled the ant farm with water, burned and tortured the ants, introduced deadly contagions and toxins and ant bullies that prey on other ants. So you never know what nasty shit he's going to spring next.

But there I was, what you might call jealous of God. And mad at him. So in the back of my mind I was thinking, "If I ever run across this asshole I just don't know what." And then it turns out he doesn't even exist. Can you believe that shit? Now whose ass do I kick?

Some atheists say that they can't be angry at God because God is not real. I say the fact that God is fictitious doesn't stop more than half the people on earth from believing in him, so why should it stop me from being mad at him? And we oughta be able to discuss him like any literary character—Astro Boy or Hannibal Lecter.

The godly say that God is everywhere, all at the same time. What if you're omni-present and don't want to be someplace? There's no place you can go where you aren't already there. And one thing you can't do if you're God is leave.

If I were trying to find God, the last place I'd look would be any of the churches I was raised in. Not unless I figured him for a tongues speaking, snake handling, frothing at the mouth, holy roller from the Ozarks. One of my people. And though I haven't been a regular churchgoer for some time, I'll explain the holy roller fundamentals for the those who haven't experienced them first-hand. And for those who have, we'll just hope this little jog down the old memory trail doesn't cause you to have some kind of post traumatic flashback.

For the Singletons, what passed for a church was a lot of times just somebody's front room or basement. A storefront was verging on ostentation. Formal worship was divided between

revivals in their various forms and church proper, which convened not just on Sunday morning,
but on Sunday, Wednesday and Friday nights.
A church revival had a guest preacher and ser-
vices every night for a week. And there were also
traveling evangelists that held revivals in everything from the giant tents that A. A. Allen and
Oral Robert hauled around in fleets of semis, to
ratty old theaters or halls rented from the Hoo
Hoos or Odd Fellows by the bottom feeders of
the proselytizing trade. When we lived out in the
country we went to brush arbor meetings. That's
where somebody throws up a makeshift tabernacle out of old road signs and scrap lumber or
whatever can be scrounged from the dump and
commences to revivalising the yokels.

Though the various holy roly congregations
of my youth often differed on particular points of
doctrine—whether there was a trinity, whether
they should baptize in this name or that, whether
the bible commanded them to take up serpents—
they were all of one mind and one accord when
it came to speaking in tongues and stumbling
around and falling on the floor, without which
you could not call yourself a holy roller. Or Pentecostal. Same thing. And tongues speaking came
in more than one form. There was the everyday
variety which went along with praying, and was
just kind of embarrassing to be around:

"And we thank thee Jesus for the victory!
Hundalashundie!"

But the worst for me were the tongues and interpretations and prophesies. Here, I'll give you a for-instance.

Bother Wagstaff jumps up and commences to giving the congregation Holy Ghost hell, a good goddamn piece of the Holy Ghost's mind. The only thing was, he'd be speaking gibberish. "Chucka latta mamma yoko! Chocalatti dunduluh furta demorka dalay! Humma showdaahlay? Shambu Barti Baba! Ash Kacky Baba! Wuh!"

Now it sounds silly when I tell it, but all the grown-ups acted like it was deadly serious, exactly as if the Holy Ghost got him a shotgun and busted in like he was robbing the place.

And don't nobody stir until somebody interprets. And what the interpreter says is just as baffling as the message in tongues.

Sister Fredonia: "Lo, sayeth the Lord thy God! Turn not away from the way that is narrow! You have turned your eyes blind! You have blinded your eyes to the blood! Lo! Lo, I say, turn not your blind eyes from way that is narrow. And the blood! Hundalashundie!"

And you could never tell what'd been eating the Holy Ghost. The Holy Ghost never had good news. The Holy Ghost never once got anybody to jump up and say, "Boy, y'all is some Christian sons of bitches. Way to fucking go." That never happened.

And sometimes, instead of going through an interpreter, the Holy Ghost might talk to the people through prophesy. No matter whose mouth he hijacked, he always spoke in something like a hillbilly's idea of King James' English.

Brother Bartholomew. He just springs to his feet right in the middle of the sermon. The more dramatic the interruption, the greater the profundity. And his eyes are closed—their eyes are always closed—and he goes off at the top of his lungs. "I am the Lord God Jehovah and lo my yoke is easy and my burden is light. But come not to me through the works of Mannon, for thou hast trespassed unto Babylon! Verily I say that the time is short and the hour is nigh!"

And, like always happens, he sits back down like he hadn't even been there when he said all that stuff.

It sure scared the shit outa me. It was weird and everybody took it seriously. And, as I say, that always scared ever damn bit of the shit right out of me. If you've never been in the middle of an old fashioned Pentecostal church service when the spirit is moving, you need to find you one and check it out. Admission's free. Think of it like a field trip. Better yet, take a hit of acid first.

Everything I've told you about until now is all mainstream by holy roly standards. But my people were snake handlers, too. We were in the minority. My grandpa, John Clarke Singleton, everybody called him Pap, preached that you could go to hell for drinking whiskey or beer, but he himself drank strychnine and bleach. He said he was going by the Gospel According to Mark. *In my name shall they cast out devils. They shall speak with new tongues. They shall take up serpents, and if they drink any deadly thing, it shall not hurt them. They shall lay hands on the sick and they shall recover.*

They laid hands on Pap when a cottonmouth water moccasin bit him in the right eye. Uncle John Travis stomped that snake to butter. And neither Pap nor the snake recovered. A cottonmouth is not a church-going snake by nature. Rattlesnakes and copperheads are about as much serpent as your average holy roller can abide, plenty enough to satisfy the letter of the gospel.

Now, I don't know if you've ever watched your own grandpa get bit in the eye by a water moccasin and die puking and pissing and shitting and crying like a little girl and rolling on the floor of a flea-bit little church way back in a holler in the middle of the night while half of everybody you know is praying for him so loud you'd think God was deaf and the other half is singing and clapping their hands and reeling around like drunks, but if you weren't scared of God before, you would be now. This was not somebody any little boy wanted to be fucking with.

You'd think that nothing could be more terrifying and damaging to a child's psyche than witnessing the sorrowful demise of his own grandpa, to say nothing of being thrown into a small room with venomous snakes and unhinged holy rollers; but scary-wise, that came in way behind watching my mamma and daddy give up their very personalities and become people I couldn't recognize, let alone count on to look after me.

The lake of fire, the grave, hell, being cut off from the love of God, the rapture, the great tribulation: all the stuff that I was supposed to be ascared of, I was. Add the snakes and the faith-healers and my folks losing their minds every time they got around God and there was still the realization that everything I thought I'd learned about compassion, humility, kindness, patience: they didn't apply to God. And we were supposed to be like him. It didn't make sense and it wasn't supposed to make sense and I was wrong to try to make it make sense. If you can find something worse than that I don't want to hear about it.

The day after Pap got snake-bit and died because nobody would take him to the hospital, I asked my mother why God just stood there without doing anything. She referred me to Chapter 2, verse 4, of Paul's First Letter to the Corinthians: *But the natural man receiveth not the things of the Spirit of God, for they are foolishness unto him. Neither can he know them. Because they are spiritually discerned.*

And we can't hope to understand except through spiritual discernment. So God really has a plan. We just don't get how God, in his great wisdom, operates. All the most horrific things you can imagine, they're all part of the plan. So relax. God's on top of it. That shit was thin when I was a boy and it's plumb wore out now.

People have been making excuses for God ever since Abraham first concocted him out of such other gods as were handy in that part of the Mideast four thousand years ago. Look at the number of books that purport to explain why God allows bad things to happen. And this has been going on since day one.

When I first heard that there was an entire field of theology called apologetics I naturally assumed that it had been set up to deal with the problem of why God is such an asshole, and why anybody with a conscience wouldn't want to avoid him like one the plagues he enjoys visiting upon his children. But no, apologetics is about defending God's existence, rather than getting him to say he's sorry. Of course, if you can't even establish that he's there, you can't expect anybody to take any of the other stuff very seriously.

You need you some faith. And the Gospel According to Benjamin Franklin says, "The way to see by faith is to shut the eye of reason." Good point, Brother Ben. Cause if you got faith, what do you want with reason? The Gospel according Merriam-Webster says, "Faith is firm belief in something for which there is no proof." If you got proof, you don't need faith. That doesn't stop some of the faithful from trying to prove God's existence. Apologetics grew up around trying to explain belief in God in ways rational people could listen to without busting out laughing. As the Gospel According to H.L. Mencken put it, trying to explain the unknowable in terms of the not worth knowing. Sorry's got nothing to do with it. God's not sorry. He's just mean.

Setting aside whether God is too cruel or lazy or disengaged to bother protecting his children from harm, you're still left with all this stuff that you might as well not even try to understand, since you can't get there through reason. That's always struck me as a sure recipe for a spiritual discernment pissing contest in which each believer says his revelation trumps his sister's or brother's.

"God showed me."

"No, he showed me, asslick."

Who was I supposed to believe? The one person I knew for a fact that God was not speaking to was me. He never said shit. I started to suspect that he never said shit to anybody else either. Even as I continued to say my prayers and tried to hang onto the naïve belief that my own personal god was on call any time to supersede the laws of nature on my behalf, I could see that he wasn't doing shit. Either he wasn't paying attention, or he wasn't up to the job. Or maybe—

I want to pause long enough to acknowledge the agnostics among us. The Gospel According to Merriam-Webster has something to say about what makes an agnostic, bless their pink little hearts. "One who is not committed to believing in either the existence or the nonexistence of God or a god." Goddamn, that doesn't sound very good. Puts me in mind of Revelation 3: *Because you are lukewarm, neither hot nor cold, I am about to spit you out of my mouth.*

But, Brother Sam, we wouldn't want to be too hasty in ruling out the goddess Isis for instance. You can't say for certain that she doesn't exist. Yep. You're agnostic alright. I'll go way the hell out on a limb and say outright that there is no Isis. No fucking Jupiter. No Zoraster, either. No God. No Jesus. No none of 'em. You go ahead on and be agnostic. Remember to set out some cookies for Santa.

The fix I got myself born into was not my fault. At least not up to a point, the point where I wanted people to stop treating me like a child. The Apostle Paul wrote in the 13th chapter of First Corinthians, *When I was a child, I spake as a child, I understood as a child, I thought as a child. But when I became a man, I put away childish things.*

I got to that stage that most teenagers go through, and some never outgrow, of being extra vigilant about letting anybody pull the wool over my eyes. My bullshit meter was fixed in the super sensitive mode. And it came to me that with an omnipotent being on the loose, every other being would have to be completely impotent. God would have every damned bit of the power. You and I would have none whatsoever. No free will. Goddamn logic. In matters of morality, a truly omnipotent god is as worthless as hair on bacon.

And even if an omnipotent god and free will were not mutually exclusive, every prayer of repentance would still be empty, would still be meaningless, would still be coerced. You can say you'd have done it anyway, but won't nobody believe you. Put yourself in God's place. How can you trust that somebody has done something willingly, because they love you or respect you, when you know that they're getting paid for it? Or that they're afraid of what'll happen if they don't play along. Again, they can say they'd have done it anyway, but goddamn. It's an uneven arrangement all around. God does not love you half as much as he wants you to love him. I pity God if the reward is absent or if you take away the threat.

My people wouldn't have liked what the Gospel According to Einstein has to say on the subject of everlasting reward and punishment. "Man would indeed be in a poor way if he had to be restrained by fear of punishment and hope of reward after death."

To hear them tell it, that was all that kept them and all their church-going friends from becoming the vilest, most depraved and debauched pestilences ever to pollute the planet. Fear of punishment was why you didn't smoke, drink, cuss, fornicate, play cards, dance, go to the movies or watch TV. And why the hell would you do anything good unless there was a reward in it for you. Every action was something of a transaction. Just don't expect the quo until you've ponied up the quid.

I'm thinking, anybody who looks to the Bible as a model for rational, just, ethical or decent behavior is fucking a dead dog. You might as well look to the Pre-Columbian Aztecs for moral guidance. The difference between the Aztecs and believers in the god of Abraham is that, thanks to some nice folks from the old country, sacramental basketball, played with the heads of those whose living hearts have been cut out before their eyes and shown to them as the last thing they ever see, is no longer recognized by the National Council of Churches, and may have died out altogether. But if Aztec nogginball is still being practiced somewhere in the world today, some folks say that I should speak of it only in terms acceptable to the athletes themselves. That bugs me. Don't make a public profession unless you want to hear back from the public.

The Bible belongs to everybody, not just the ones that treat it as their own family album. Anybody who won't even bother to read the whole thing should have the good grace to refrain from pontificating until they have. My people like to make out like they're some kind of biblical authorities, but they just pick at it like picky little buzzards, careful to take only the parts that agree with them, the parts they can swallow whole and regurgitate without digesting. By god, they know the bible means what it says and says what it means, even if they don't know what it says, let alone what it means.

So I tried to get my cousin Palmer, he's my Uncle John Wesley's middle boy, and was attending Roberts Oral University at the time, to admit that the god he worshipped was a limited one, a god-lite, some kind of little old low-fat god, since God either has all the power or he doesn't. That switch is either on or it's off. There is no third position. The best Palmer could come up with was that God gave humans enough free will to decide for themselves whether to accept him or not, and how to behave. But he was still omnipotent.

When I pointed out to Palmer that he was as good as saying that God is only relatively omnipotent, he just said he'd pray for me. And I still did not slap that boy.

Free will is hard. You got to decide things for yourself. Belief in God is a voluntarily self-inflicted intellectual lobotomy, performed by stuffing your cranium with toxic sawdust that crowds out brain cells and eats away IQ points.

Everybody has heard the quote from the Gospel According to Voltaire about how if there were no God it would be necessary to invent one.

Remember what the Gospel According to Jean Paul Sartre says about that? How even if God existed it would be necessary to deny him, since the very notion of God negates freedom? You're goddamn right, Brother J.P. Of course, that's exactly what some people want, isn't it? Freedom is scary. Especially other people's freedom. We don't want to be free and we can't have you being free either.

For some folks being God's livestock represents a kind of freedom. Not just from personal responsibility, since an omnipotent god means no free will, but from rules of all kinds. Don't like natural laws? Suspend them. Can't get a definition to jibe with your position? Just make up some shit. You never have to tax your brain trying to figure out how stuff works, because God is behind everything. There is no question that you don't already know the answer to. Cheap fantasy is seductive, but stupid.

Stupid? That's a mighty harsh word and I don't like using it. I just don't have a better one to describe betting everything you've got on the hearsay promise of a payoff that can't be collected until you're dead.

Palmer asked me, "Don't you want to go to heaven?" I told him, hell no. Everybody in heaven is either an idiot or an asshole, cause once you're there, you cease giving ary a shit. All the loved ones you were so worried about back on earth? Fuck 'em. I got mine. It has to be that way or it wouldn't be heaven, would it? You can't have grief or regret intruding on your bliss, or what'd be the point? Nope. It's Burn in hell, losers. And I don't care if you were my baby, my husband, wife, parent, friend. The selfishness is complete, there is no more to be desired. It's like the imaginary forty virgins that suicide bombers get their puny little peckers in a peak over.

Goddamn. See if you haven't come across this one. I was talking to Palmer again, and this was just the other day, and I must've said goddamn without even noticing it. I do that. I've always been partial to goddamn. And Palmer starts in on me about how since I used the Lord's name in vain, I must believe in God. Well, I reminded Palmer about how Proverbs 26 says *Answer not a fool according to his folly.* Why the hell should anybody, believer or no, give one curly little hair on a red rat's ass whether anybody else is an atheist? Or feel the need to convince them they're not. Or worse, tell them that atheism is just another brand of belief. Atheism is not a religion. It is not a cult. It is to belief in God what a vacuum is to air. The absence of theism. If you sucked all the belief in God out of the universe, what you'd have left is atheism. And far less methane gas being released into the atmosphere.

I got more to say about goddamn. When Clark Kent's editor at the Daily Planet, Perry White, says "Great Caesar's Ghost!" he's not actually invoking the specter of Julius Caesar, any more than saying holy cow causes sanctified bovines to pop into existence. So I'm going to go on saying goddamn. I say it with a little g, but it's okay if you hear it with a big G.

I'm pretty much going to stay off politics to-night, other than to note that God is a parasitic slime mold that has been sucking the brains out of the U.S.A. since before its founding. The Europeans tracked it over on those shoes with the big buckles on 'em. Over the past 400 years it's worked its way into all the cracks and crannies of American life. And we're not just talking about "In God We Trust" on the money. Every public school, courthouse, city hall: the federal courts: the government itself. They reek of God, got God smeared all over them. I resent the hell out my taxes being used to promote God's brand name.

In God We Trust. The Gospel According Mark Twain says it wouldn't sound any better if it were true. It's like the government has to keep reminding me that I'm permanently relegated to America's hind tit just because I don't buy into that shit. You ever think about the number of times you're exposed to the word "god" in the course of a day? We gotta start paying closer attention, noticing when God shows up uninvited. Every "In God We Trust," every "One nation under God," every Ten Commandments monument, every prayer that opens a session of a legislature, every federal observance of a Christian holiday. Not that we should get fewer days off, but we ought to be able to get them without celebrating our own marginalization.

These state-sponsored professions of belief are designed to calm the insane. Reminding the rest of us that we're merely visitors on the ward is what you'd call an ancillary benefit.

The Constitution guarantees even the pathologically delusional the freedom to speak any nonsense they like. And what they do in the privacy of their own loony bins is their business, so long as it's all between consenting adults— and they leave the children out of it. And they don't prevail upon the likes of Brother Sam to pick up their tax burden. The government already underwrites their programming and does their P.R. for free. You buy, sell, or rent out property, and you are a business. Pay your fucking share you deadbeat parasites.

And when citizens that do pay taxes try to pass laws that require these civic leeches to chip into to the community pot, who decides the outcome? A bunch of legislators who could never get elected without professing belief in God. Nobody cares that the Gospel According to Article Four of the Constitution says, "No religious test shall ever be required as a qualification to any office or public trust under the United States." The problem isn't with the Constitution, it's with the voters.

Of course, you can always turn to the courts.

You'll know the building by the bigass Ten Commandments out front. The very courthouse where Sister Singleton and I go to do our county business has one. I bet yours does, too.

God forbid that you should ever be accused of a crime or have to rely on the fairness of a jury or judge in a civil proceeding. If the bailiff asks you to swear that the testimony you are about to give is the truth so help you God, are you gonna call the proceedings to a halt so you can explain that you can't swear to a god you don't believe in? So you can make a point of being a member of the one minority that political correctness hasn't gotten to yet? If you got any sense you'll say, "Hell yes! I swear before God, Jehovah, Yaweh, the Almighty, he whose name must not be spoken, the Father, Son, and Holy Ghost. Praise his holy name. That Ninth Commandment posted outside the front door there commands me to not bear false witness against my neighbor, and that's flat what I'm not gonna do. You bet I swear to God. By God."

Swearing an oath before God is the nod and wink that tells the government that you can be trusted to join the military or preside over a court, serve in congress, the White House, state house, or city council. You're one of them. You promise not to call bullshit on the whole deal.

I may be willing to be mad at a god that does not exist, but that's it. I'm goddamned if I'm gonna fear God. Sure, some of his people bear watching, but I'm no more afraid of God than I am of the this Flying Spaghetti Monster deal. But that isn't to say there's nothing left worth worrying about. You want to know what causes old Brother Sam to wake up in a cold sweat at a quarter to noon and not be able to get back to sleep again even with the 700 Club on in the background? It's knowing that this enthusiastic embrace of the improbable, this obstinate fidelity to falsehood, is damn near an absolute requirement for the highest offices in the most powerful government in human history. It scares the bejeesus out of me that the people entrusted with our very lives are avowed fantasists: card carrying, full-fledged, year-round residents of Wonderland who use our taxes not only to shove big wads of God up our asses, but to wage sectarian war in our name, as if it's us Christians and Jews against those Moslems.

I want it understood: Brother Sam does not throw in with sanctimonious thugs and pious bullies. And I don't give the first shit which fairy tale they favor.

The Gospel According to Voltaire also says, "If we believe absurdities, we shall commit atrocities." You want absurd? Imagine a universe without mysteries, a universe that's a closed book. I'll tell you one thing for goddamned sure, no one ever learned anything from a closed book, no matter how good it's supposed to be. Atrocities?

Start with torturing logic and language, but save the most depraved shit for infidels—fellow believers. Not that actual heathens, nonbelievers like Brother Sam, shouldn't be maltreated. That's what minorities are for.

I'll grant that not all believers are as extreme as the ones that raised me. Or those that put out a contract on a cartoonist. Or tell women or homosexuals that they're not good enough or smart enough and don't have a right to personal freedom. But, near as I can figure, once you take that initial step off the deep end of reason, and accept God on nothing but faith, you're down to splitting hairs over whether the Sugar Plum Fairy has buckles or bells on her shoes. You might as well grab a rattlesnake with one hand and a bottle of rat poison with the other and kick up a Holy Ghost cancan to hosannas sung in unknown tongues.

"Whoa!" I heard somebody say. Brother Sam you done committed one giant-assed generalization, heaping all believers together that way.

I know.

IF THE OCEAN WAS WHISKEY
AND GOD WAS A DUCK

Goddamn. One thing I learned from listening to my godly kin trying to explain away evolution and physics and geology is that the dumber you are, the more things make sense.

Comes a time as a child when you begin to suspect that maybe your folks do not actually know everything. Then you get to thinking maybe you do. That was little Brother Sam at nine. But you don't have to be a genius to figure out the most obvious thing in the world, namely, that there is no God. So being an atheist does not necessarily put you in line for the Nobel Prize. Of course, it helps. Look at Einstein. And Mother Teresa.

That phase of mistaking myself for a great thinker passed some time ago. These days I find it hard to credit my thinking as superior to anybody else's. If I can figure this stuff out, surely most anybody can.

One thing for certain is that nobody begins life a theist. That's why Brother Sam is always

going on about reversion to the natural a-the-
istic state into which we all are born. You can't
get to be a theist without somebody deliberately
tricking you into believing in God.

For me, reversion—that's the opposite of conversion—took about ten years. The process started when I was four and learned to read. From
that point, God's days were numbered, although
neither of us knew it. I was fourteen when I read
the Kings James Version of the Bible all the way
through, which did God in for good. Put him out
of my misery. Goddamn.

And before I get going, I'll just explain to
anybody heretofore unacquainted with Brother
Sam's ways, that me saying goddamn does not
indicate that I believe there's an actual god doing any actual damning. It's ironic. Like the term
"Atheist Evangelist." Goddamn.

As a youth I subjected my folks, Maureen
Sedgwick Singleton and John Calvin Singleton,
all three of my father's brothers, John Wesley,
John Travis, and John Fletcher Singleton, their
wives, my Aunts Winnie, Chestina, and Ethylene,
everybody, to the same ceaseless questioning.
That got to wearing thin, or so I gathered.

I asked my father, "Could God beat up Superman?" He said, "There is no Superman. Superman is just made up." And, as was usual,
he quoted some Bible at me. "'Titus 3:9. '*But
avoid foolish questions, and genealogies, and*

contentions, and strivings about the law; for they are unprofitable and vain.'"

I knew better than to back-sass either him or the Bible. So I put most of my questions directly to God, and went to writing them down in this little book. I got it from my mother, who bought it to put recipes in but never did, probably because about the only things she ever got to cook were fried potatoes, cornbread, and pinto beans, and she knew how to make them by heart. I asked God, if he loved me as much as everybody said he did, how come he made me live with people who ate mainly beans. That was one of the things that got me to doubting God in the first place.

That book became a record of my relationship with God till I fired him off his job for not showing up. And the record was all in the form of questions.

I carried my book with me everywhere. When somebody asked, I would explain that it was full of these questions for God. My folks actually thought that was a good thing. Of course, they never read the questions, so far as I know.

Now, they had already warned me that God does not enjoy being tested. They told me, if there's one thing gives God the gripes, it's some measly little human trying to put him on the spot. He has been known to do some smiting, you go too far down that road. So watch it. I was not looking to start up with God. I was just asking simple, sincere questions like the child I was.

I started with something easy to see how God did with that. I wrote, "Do you know how to swim?"

Of course, there being no God, there likewise was no answer. Don't expect me to point out every time there is no answer from God. No God. No answers. In the absence of better intelligence, I marked God down as not knowing how to swim.

My father's usual reply to my questions amounted to: "Because I said so," or "Because God said so." And the distinction between my father's word and the word of God was insignificant. Neither provided so much as one anemic little candle-power of illumination. I decided that "Because I said so" counted as "Don't ask me." And "Because God said so" counted as "Don't ask him, either." Of course, I did.

I was nine when I was rooting around in the library and came across my first paradox, the one that goes, "Could God create a stone so big he couldn't lift it?" I found it a fascinating question, so I repeated it to my father. He said, "'*But foolish and unlearned questions avoid, knowing that they do gender strifes.*' Second Timothy 2:23."

Another time, I came home from school and had just learned about evaporation and condensation. Now, I knew for a fact, or up to that time believed I knew, that there was no such thing as rain before the Great Flood. So I asked my father if that meant there was no water cycle and he got mad and told me to go read Genesis. So I did.

Boringest thing I had ever read. Made me wonder if learning to read was worth it. I asked God, "Does the Bible get any better?"

There's an old saying: "You can lead a horse to water, but you've gotta go upside his head with a two-by-four if you don't want him to drink." That is exactly analogous to my folks letting me learn to read. And what they went upside little Sam's head with was the Bible. And sometimes when they didn't want to bother with one of my questions, they'd just say, "Write it down in your book."

And I did. Here's one: "How much toilet paper can you take before it's stealing?"

I was just winding up fourth grade right there in Kansas City—the real one, Kansas City, Missouri—at the time I commenced this keeping tabs on God. Some time before the end of the school year my father moved us back to Texas County where he spent his youth being moved around by his father, who spent his youth being moved around by his father, and so unto the earliest Singletons, the proto- or cave-Singletons, who even as far back as the dawn of the Ozarks could neither stay put nor hold a job, but who felt led of the Lord to preach.

That spring I saw my grandfather get bit in the eye by a water moccasin and die at church. And, yes, I did have some questions about that, some of which I have previously reported in the hard-edged investigative journalism piece entitled Sam Singleton, Atheist Evangelist, Patriarchs and Penises. And since where I come from we only chew our cabbage once, I will refrain from restating them here.

No sooner had we settled in than my father quit his job hauling stave bolts to the cooperage when his payroll check bounced. He said it was the Lord's will because the staves went to making whiskey barrels and having anything to do with making whiskey was a terrible sin.

We lived on Mud Lick Road, which follows Paw-Paw Creek through Tick Holler, in a place we were renting for thirty dollars a month, eight miles out of Success. When we moved in there was chicken shit all over the floor, but no actual chickens, the chickens obviously having decided they deserved better. The water came out of a cistern and couldn't be trusted. There was no indoor plumbing. The privy was uphill and leaned so we worried that it might break loose and wind up down in the kitchen with one of us in it.

We did have electric and a phone on the party line, but were way behind on both. And Old Man Clintwood, who owned the place, was telling us we'd have to move if we couldn't make up two months of back rent, which I knew my folks never had any intention of paying. In fact, we always moved in the middle of the night.

Dirty Gerty had this little country store over at Plato. She let my folks buy gas and groceries on credit till she couldn't carry them anymore. My father said, "She can wait. I'd druther owe it to you forever than do you out of it."

Pinto beans were nineteen cents a pound. Gasoline was nineteen cents a gallon. And unless somebody got to bringing in something quick, the Singletons were going to be in a gasless condition.

It was late that summer that the Lord got to burdening my father's heart awful bad over the lost souls of Texas County. About how if somebody with a mighty call to preach didn't set himself to some soul winning, most of the locals were either gonna die lost or have to sit out the Rapture.

And thus, too, sayeth the Lord, "John Calvin Singleton, I am herewith commanding you to hold a revival, in particular, a brush arbor meeting, as in the days of old."

The Lord said people would flock to a brush arbor meeting as in the days of old, but did not provide any further details aside from a firm insistence that it be convened on Birch Blake's place. This epiphany came unto my father of a Sunday afternoon.

Some people say that God is inscrutable, that he works in mysterious ways his wonders to perform, which is nicer than just coming right out and saying he's an idiot. Well, picking Birch Blake's place for a revival was strange, even for God. Maybe he was figuring how Birch was the only one we knew who owned land, and therefore the only one who could provide the site for the brush arbor. But Birch Blake cooked whiskey on his land, or had till he got one to three in Jeff City for beating up his wife Bernace.

The way that happened was, one night, like so many nights before, Birch whipped Bernace and passed out. Only this time Bernace tied him up by his ankles and dragged him all the way to the bottom of the hill behind his three-quarter ton truck, which she then set afire. Birch wound up in the hospital for five days, and went directly from the sick ward to the jailhouse, then to the penitentiary. With Birch in the p-farm, Sheriff Glen Puckett found in himself the courage to wreck the three thumper stills whose general whereabouts on the Blake place had always been an open secret. When Birch got sprung after eighteen months, his operation was in ruins. Of course Bernace was there waiting for him.

The Blakes and the Singletons went back generations, the Blakes living and moonshining on land they owned, the Singletons living and preaching on land somebody else owned. Although the latter saw leading the former unto the path of righteousness as their sacred commission, nary a Blake had ever found Jesus, so far as anybody knew. Never even looked. For my father and his brothers, bagging a Blake would mean accomplishing that which none of their forebears named John Singleton had done.

One thing I remember about Birch. He drank from a tin can which seemed bonded to his hand, in that I never saw him put it down even once. I always figured he had to have pounded Bernace one-handed. I didn't know how he ever got his overalls hitched up.

Now, my uncle John Wesley lived over in Houston. He, too, was unemployed and hard up and had felt led of the lord do a little soul winning and see didn't some love offerings start coming in. He called my father on the telephone that same Sunday and they got to comparing notes on their respective leadings of the Lord and settled on a collaborative approach on the brush arbor, which boiled down to Uncle John Wesley providing his flatbed truck, his gas, and his tools, Birch Blake providing his land, and my father providing his epiphany.

Uncle John Wesley said, "That old reprobate never did nothing for nobody in his entire life without there was something in it for him. And I don't mean the sweet satisfaction of a deed well done, neither."

My father said, "The Lord will make a way," although the Lord never had, and never did, and never will, make a way or anything else. Like the Bible says, he is the same yesterday, today, and forever.

So Uncle John Wesley came by first thing Monday morning and we all went over to break the news to Birch. I could tell right off that Birch was not especially receptive to the proposition of a brush arbor being thrown up out in front of his house, or a bunch of Holy Rollers rolling around all over the place being holy, cause he flat said so.

"It wouldn't look good. I gotta be careful about my reputation."

Then, like he'd suddenly had some big change of heart, he said to my father, "Tell you what, John Calvin, since Bernace burned down my three-quarter ton truck, I have no way of picking up this load of car parts this guy's holding for me up to Rolla. If you boys could run up there and get 'em—"

My father said "Why, that's no problem atall." Uncle John Wesley didn't say a thing.

Birch said, "You get me them parts and maybe we can talk some more about this bushy harbor of yours." He belched pungently. Said, "Goddammit, cheated myself out of a fart."

So we drove up to Rolla and the scrap yard guy looked at us like we were criminals and showed us this pile of rusty radiators. I asked Uncle John Wesley what in the Sam Hill Birch Blake could possibly want with a truckload of old radiators.

"I'd say he was fixing to make him a still," he said to me. "And it'd have be a big one. And I don't mean small."

My father said, "Son, we do not know for sure what old Birch is fixing to do with these radiators."

No matter what my father said, I was

absolutely charmed to think that I might in some way be helping to bring an actual moonshine still into being. I asked my father if he had ever drunk whiskey. He didn't say anything, but Uncle John Wesley said how when they were not much older than I was, the two of them used to go up to the Blake place when Birch's dad, old Oscar, was putting up jugs and he'd look away while they snuck a swaller. He started to tell me some more when my father cut him off. "John Wesley, you can go to hell the same for lying as you can for stealing."

But I was fascinated. Of course, I did not even know at the time that whiskey is just distilled beer, and that beer— Well, as you know, beer is responsible for what we think of as civilization.

Birch had traded the ruins of his copper stills for these forty-seven car radiators, free-on-board, Rolla. We got them loaded on the flatbed and arrived at Birch's place just after three in the p.m. He led us to an overgrown knob in this grove of white oaks and said, "Well one other thing is somebody'd have to get a bush hog up here and get after this Johnson grass. That'd be part of the bargain. That's for goddamn sure. And I'd say that and them radiators'd be worth no more'n a week. I'll give you boys seven days."

My father knew that Uncle John Travis had a bush hog. He said, "Birch, I can have a bush hog up here first thing in the morning. So just don't you worry about that. And as far as a week goes, why, in a week's time Joshua fit the battle of Jericho and the walls came a-tumblin' down. Before a week from now you might could find salvation your own self."

Birch said, "Cram it, John Calvin. One goddamn week. And the bush hogging in advance."

The next morning we drove up to Licking to conscript Uncle John Travis. I say conscript because he made absolutely clear that he was not volunteering either himself or his bush hog. But his brothers wouldn't take no. We got the bush hog and its operator aboard and were down to the Blake place before ten.

While Birch was laying out the particulars of the bush hogging, I wandered off to look for arrowheads and turned up a huge rattlesnake. So I asked if they were going to save it for church. Before anybody could say word one, Uncle John Travis grabbed a post and reduced that snake to a uniform paste.

Uncle John Wesley said, "John Travis, I believe the Lord led you to mash that rattlesnake that way. The Lord is leading us Singletons to lay down the serpent and let it go. Our debt has been wiped clean by the precious blood of the lamb and Pap's, too. '*By grace are ye saved not of works lest any man should boast.*'"

My father said amen. The bush hogging and snake slaying and amenning were about the only things that got done on Tuesday. I asked the

Lord to leave me out of it the next time he wanted a snake slayed.

I'll admit I had a fascination for reptiles, still do, but it has always stopped short of having the least desire to carry on exactly as you could imagine a herpetologist warning you not to do. "By no means should you ever grab a pit viper and shake it around in a small room where people are speaking in tongues and waving their arms and stumbling all over the place."

And yes, I recognize that only a tiny percentage of the fringe-most Pentecostals are steady snake waggers. But as Brother Sam says, "Once you accept God on nothing but faith, you're down to splitting hairs over whether the Sugar Plum Fairy has buckles or bells on her shoes. You might as well grab a rattlesnake with one hand and a bottle of rat poison with the other and kick up a Holy Ghost can-can to hosannas sung in unknown tongues." Plus, snake handling was what my people did.

After I watched Pap get bit and die at church, God equaled death. Senseless cruel death. Like the Rapture wasn't worrisome enough. I now also knew from first-hand observation that God would as soon kill you as look at you. Kill you horribly. Right in front of everybody. I asked God who was next, and next time couldn't he go with something a little less— gruesome, like a crucifixion?

The late Pap, John Clark Singleton, preached

brush arbors back in the '20s and '30s, in these very hills, alongside his brothers: John Bunyan, John Mulkey, John Broadus, and John Gill Singleton. It was obviously way before my time, but I gathered that their arbors were actually made from brush. I'd heard the term "brush arbor" my entire life and had always pictured a pretty little structure of boughs and branches, open on the sides, filled with happy hillbillies praising the Lord and singing happy little songs about all the things you can do with blood, providing it's Jesus's blood, or as they put it, the precious blood of the lamb. You can wash in it. Launder your robes in it. You can jump around in a fountain filled with it. And boy does it catch fish.

Anyway, blood was the main thing they enjoyed singing about and they had about a hundred songs, all about blood, which gave me the creeps.

I could tell right after Uncle John Wesley picked my father and me up at seven Wednesday morning to go out to the County Dump that brush was not going to enter into the making of this arbor. They were fixing to pitch them a trash arbor unto the Lord.

We rooted up some bent and rusty sheets of corrugated tin, what looked like one side of an orange and blue truck trailer, an assortment of rusted-out buckets and tubs, and a slab of barn wood with a *Mail Pouch Tobacco* sign painted on it. We helped ourselves to some wide boards which we found stacked behind a shed, but had to hurry before anybody came along.

It reminded me of when one of us had worms and my father would go in search of a peach tree my mother could make peach tree tea with. He always waited till the middle of the night. The same with roastin' ears, or as I've heard some people call 'em, corn on the cob. The whole time I was coming up, I never ate a single roastin' ear that wasn't appropriated from a roadside crop. Nobody ever talked about that being stealing, but they were awfully careful to make sure the farmer wasn't watching.

I recognized the inconsistency with what I'd been told about "Thou shalt not steal," and I fretted about my folks placing their immortal souls in peril. Later, I figured out how they must have claimed an *Eighth Commandment* exemption based on the time Jesus put a couple of his disciples up to rustling a donkey. Remind me to get back to the donkey.

The only possible site on the Blake place for the brush arbor was on the clearing right out there in front of the house, not fifty yards from Birch and Bernace's door. Permission to put up even a temporary tabernacle on that spot was a hell of a thing to ask. Especially from Birch Blake, who if you saw him, you would instantly recognize as no Holy Roller. That is, if you could make him out through the fumes coming off that can he never turned loose of.

You'd think an old man whose nightly habit was to drink himself mean and stupid would be a late riser, but not so. That morning, when we pulled up in front of his house just before nine, Birch looked at our load of materials and said, "I appreciate you boys stopping by on your way to the dump. Let me see can't I find something needs hauled off, too."

We pulled the stuff off the flatbed. My job was to go through and separate any boards that had nails in them and pull the nails out and straighten them, since there was no money for nails. I asked the Lord if swiping something crummy was any less sinful than swiping something good.

The three John Singletons argued without ceasing over everything from which end to put the platform on, to whether the *Mail Pouch Tobacco* sign should face in or out, seeing as how using tobacco in any form was a sin, and they didn't want to it look like they were advertising. They settled on an inward-facing sign, turned upside down.

Uncle John Travis had been backslid ever since Pap's death from Holy Ghost related snakebite. And when he showed up late on Wednesday everybody was mad at him till he opened his trunk and produced this big watermelon. Which they never asked the origin of. He volunteered how on his way to the house yesterday he come across these watermelons just sitting in this field. So he picked this one and left it in the creek overnight so we could enjoy it today. Uncle John Travis was always generous like that.

I do not like watermelon. I do not even like the smell. So I screwed up my courage and took the wedge Uncle John Travis gave me and carried it up to Birch. He took a big bite, chased it with a swig from his can, and spit a seed on my shoe. My father hollered at me and I ran back down and resumed pulling nails. He and his brothers were back to fussing, which, as Aunt Ethylene said, was how they got their enjoys.

By two the next afternoon, that was Thursday, the brush arbor was as done as it was ever gonna get. And everybody was in high spirits. When Uncle John Wesley asked, "You got the victory, John Calvin?" my father shouted "Amen!"

I personally did not feel safe standing under it. It was plain that just because Jesus was a hand with carpentry did not mean his followers were too. There ought to be a general law of construction which says, "First consider gravity." Maybe there is. If so, my father and uncles never heard about it. Or they didn't believe in it. "The Bible doesn't say anything about gravity."

Finally, when this abomination unto architecture had attained completeness, a Zen-like tension between heap of shit and holy temple, Birch came over to my father and said, he said, "Goddamn, John Calvin. It ain't everybody can make trash look worse, but you boys done 'er. Y'all got a week like I agreed. That is if this here deal don't fall down and kill somebody first. She looks like she's got maybe three days in her, don't come no wind or rain. One goddamn week."

He had again stood right there and said goddamn to my father's face. I had long since lost track of the times I heard my father jump salty on somebody, very often a complete stranger, for taking the Lord's name in vain. Violating the very first commandment.

"You say that and you might as well be calling me a filthy name." And he wasn't kidding, either. Made it a matter of who was going to back down. Was prepared to take measures. He liked to say, "If you won't stick up for God, you can't expect him to stick up for you."

But here's bleary-eyed drunk old Birch Blake saying goddamn and neither my father nor Uncle John Wesley, who is exactly the same way, says word one. The way my father flinched when Birch said it, imbued that goddamn with uncommon power. Goddamn. It frightened and delighted me. I resolved to someday make it my own. And so to me, these many years later, goddamn still signifies liberation and still makes me happy every time I say it. Can I get a goddamn? Goddamn.

I couldn't help but see Birch's getting away with saying goddamn, not only in front of my father and uncle, but, worse, in front of me, as evidence of a double standard. Why should he get to say it when nobody else could? I'd never even thought about saying goddamn up to that point, but once I did let the idea enter my mind, the only image that came to me was my father knocking me into the next county while simultaneously schooling me on Scripture as I sailed backward through the air.

"'*Thou shalt not take the name of the Lord thy God in vain: for the Lord will not hold him guiltless that taketh his name in vain.*'"

Something unfair was going on here. And you didn't have to be any great thinker to see what it was. My father wanted something from Birch. One week. Goddamn.

My father also wanted something from the area's preachers. It is customary for an evangelist to extend the hand of fellowship to the indigenous Holy Rollers. Pastor Jones announces the revival from the pulpit and encourages his congregation to attend. He gets to sit on the platform at the revival.

Pentecostal pastors from miles around strove to be among the spotlighted phalanx behind the pulpit of A.A. Allen or Oral Robert, the two biggest tent evangelists of the time. Saggy socks and shiny shinbones. You could smell the Brylcreme from ten rows back. They'd sit up there with their chests puffed out so as to best show off their red silk A.A. Allen or Oral Robert Supporting Pastor ribbons, like they all came in second place at the county fair.

But a low-grade Ozarkian exhorter surnamed Singleton had to scrounge for pastoral patronage. Thursday afternoon was spent calling on men of the cloth.

We knew of five Pentecostal churches within about a half-hour's drive of the Blake place: the Burning Bush Church of God with Signs Following, which was where Pap got bit and died, and not a one of us had been back since. An Assembly of God, crossed off for being too modernistic, a United Pentecostal, eliminated outright for being Oneness, which I'd just as soon not get into, a Bible Way Fellowship, known as the Consecrated Church of the Soul Cleansing Blood of the Lamb, that met in a defunct body shop and was pastored by Jimmy Dunnigan, who had been to bible college and never let anybody forget it, which, if you knew my father—

Brother Dunnigan was from Arkansas and had a great big wife named Wanda. He said he felt that Lord wanted him to preach one night of the revival and to superintend every night. Plus, the Lord wanted Wanda to be the song leader.

Now, that was a problem since Aunt Winnie had already called dibs on it. My father and Uncle John Wesley talked it over and decided that Brother Dunnigan and the Lord must've got their wires crossed. They told him, "We feel that the Lord is leading us in another direction." Which, to me, sounded a lot like "Go to hell."

The Pressed Down and Shaken Together Full

Gospel Tabernacle of Praise and Glory Everlasting was officially nondenominational, although it was doctrinally aligned with the Pentecostal Holiness Church, which in Missouri and Arkansas goes as the Church of You Don't Need Snakes to Scare the Shit out of Children. This branch had been formed by and was still under the pastorship of Hobart Delbarton.

We went over there for morning worship one time. It smelled of mildew and Ben Gay. And though it was a cloudless summer Sunday, and the windows and doors were wide open, a funereal darkness pervaded that place. The congregation looked as if they'd showed up for church forty years ago and never had the energy to leave. The addition of an electric chair would have brightened it up considerably.

Brother Delbarton was about a hundred years old and had big yellow teeth and gray skin. I looked at him and thought: the Preacher from the Black Lagoon. He preached against TV and bowing down before the rabbit-eared altar of Baal. You'd think that a tirade like that would at least be entertaining, but coming out of spooky old Preacher Delbarton it was dry as a popcorn poot.

Every time I heard somebody tell about TV, it just made me wish we had one. I asked my father if watching TV was a sin before TV was invented. He said, "Write it down in your book. Besides, we can't afford a TV set."

Sam Singleton, Atheist Evangelist

When we went to see Brother Delbarton about getting him to throw his support behind the brush arbor meeting, he said he felt led of the Lord, not only to endorse the revival, but to offer up this piano.

Somebody had just donated a newer one to his church and now this ancient upright needed to be gotten rid of. "Y'all can have it for coming to haul it off. Just so you know you can't bring it back. It's yours for keeps, praise Jesus."

The revival was set to begin at seven-thirty Friday night. Uncle John Wesley pulled up at a quarter past. Then Brother Delbarton and the contingent from the Pressed Down and Shaken Together Full Gospel Tabernacle of Praise and Glory Everlasting straggled in. Bob the egg man, who was driving by, stopped to see what was going on, mistaking the brush arbor for a rummage sale. That brought the number of attendees to twenty-one. And Bob left right after the opening prayer.

Aunt Winnie got to be the song leader. This guy nobody knew played spoons. Aunt Ethylene played the piano, which was out of tune but sounded sweet. So, too, did Uncle John Travis on his guitar and Uncle John Wesley on his mandolin. When they sang with my father? It was beautiful.

We had just gotten into *Pow'r in the Blood* when I smelled perfume and there was a rustle from the seat behind mine. I sort of ducked my chin to the left just a dab and snuck a quick reconnoiter back there. It was Bernace Blake.

After *Are You Washed in the Blood* and *Nothing but the Blood*, Uncle John Wesley asked Brother Delbarton to lead the Testimony Service and he turned it into a chance to do a little preaching of his own, a breach of Holy Roller protocol, which limits testimonies to a minute or so of telling how God has been especially good to you within the past few days, with allowances made for messages in tongues, "Hundalashundie," and like that. Brother Delbarton went on for ten minutes about how folks were not doing enough foot washing at church, per John 13: verses 14 and 15.

"Jesus said, *'If I then, your Lord and Master, have washed your feet; ye also ought to wash one another's feet. For I have given you an example, that ye should do as I have done to you.'"*

I could tell that he was trying to incite a foot washing service right then and there. I looked at that gray skin and those yellow teeth and tried not to think about his bare feet.

I was relieved when Uncle John Wesley moved on to the prayer requests. After the offering, Aunt Winnie and Uncle John Wesley sang a special, *Saved Thro' Jesus' Blood*. She sat back down and he stayed at the pulpit, which he had bought at an army surplus store the year before.

He said, *"'For where two or three are gathered together in my name, there am I in the midst of them.*"' And after pausing for everybody to amen him, he moved right on to the sermon proper, which took exception to the song *Wait a Little Longer, Please Jesus.* As some of y'all know, there's a line in there: "—just a few more days to get our loved ones in." His theme was that that was more than his loved ones deserved. "Come ahead on, Jesus. Let's get this Rapture underway. Any of my loved ones ain't ready, to hell with 'em."

It may not sound scary the way I put it, but the thought that my loved ones might miss the Rapture worried me about to death. I knew I was OK. But my folks? I lived with 'em. And I didn't like their chances.

The drills we did at school, in case an atom bomb got dropped on us, already kept me somewhat on edge, but there were no drills for the Rapture. No duck and cover and sizzle. There would be no twenty minutes in which to form a circle and kiss each other's asses goodbye.

Getting in on the Rapture, while everybody with more income and more education missed out was the main reason for being a Holy Roller. That, and getting to release the screaming lunatic inside your head any time the spirit moved. The grown-ups never ceased talking—hollering—about how the Rapture was gonna happen at any minute. It was absolutely imminent.

So when Uncle John Wesley got to the altar call, and asked Aunt Ethylene to play *There is a Fountain Filled with Blood*, and his voice got very quiet and serious and earnest, I was anxious that my folks repent their many sins while the repenting was good.

He said, "I want everybody to close their eyes, praise Jesus. Just close your eyes. Now, with every head bowed and every eye closed, I want you to ask yourself, if Jesus came tonight would you be ready? If you have any doubt whether you would be called away with the saints, I want you to raise your hand. Nobody will see you. There's a hand. Praise Jesus. Who else? Amen. Now, anybody raised their hand, just come on up and Jesus will meet you at the cross."

After a little Uncle John Travis came down and knelt at the altar where everybody, my folks included, crowded around him while he got right with the Lord. They prayed him straight through to the Holy Ghost. It took about a half-hour, though it seemed like all night. But he wound up with his trembling hands raised high, bawling like a baby and babbling streams of tongues. "Humma showdaahlay? Shambu Barti Baba!" I was embarrassed for him. And even more worried for my folks.

When we got to milling around after the service, as church-goers will do, Bernace had already headed back to the house. We could hear Birch in there, giving her hell.

The talk on the way home went from how wonderful it was to see John Travis prayed through, to how the offering was only two dollars and sixteen cents and they had to split it with Uncle John Wesley, who felt he should get it all because he preached.

That's when my mother announced that she thought little Sam should preach the Sunday night service.

You see, from the day I first formed sounds into words, I was a talker. Windy. Some grownup was always saying how I was windy. Didn't make a lick of difference. Talk talk talk, that was me. So, as I say, my folks came up with the idea that what seemed like an exceedingly annoying personal fault was in fact an exceedingly annoying gift from God. What it was was a call to preach.

When my mother told me that I was to preach the Sunday night service, the first concern that entered my head was not about having to prepare and deliver a sermon, it was about my clothes. I was ashamed of my wardrobe. And here's the odd part. Even though I was born without a normal fear of public speaking, I could be rendered inert by embarrassment over my attire. My folks knew this; they did not even try to understand it, let alone accommodate it. In fact, it pissed them off. I knew what I would have to wear, a pair of rust-colored corduroys which had been worn shiny by their previous owner, my cousin Palmer, and a green plaid shirt that was way small.

The drive home took about ten minutes. Before we arrived I had already flatly refused to be subjected to that particular torture. My father said they'd see about that. I went to bed mad.

I woke up mad Saturday morning. I was eating my taters and kinda pouting, as a child will do, and my mother said to me, she said, "All you really need is a pair of pants and a shirt. How about if we was take you up to Lazy Larry's this afternoon and let you pick out your own?"

My father looked up and said, "We was thinking you and Palmer might want to pass out tracts and do a little witnessing over to Houston and try and turn out some people for tonight."

I wanted those clothes. But what was this about spending my Saturday way over in Houston accosting total strangers on the street, with Palmer no less. I agreed, but I was still mad.

My father said, "Wife! Get Winnie on the phone and tell her we need Palmer to go witnessing over to Houston with Sam. We'll be by to get him directly we can get there. Tell her to feed him."

So we picked up Palmer. He's eleven months older than I am and has always acted like that makes him some kind of hot shot. My father just dropped us off with our handfuls of tracts. He said he'd be back in a couple of hours and to look for him driving around the square.

The whole day, I got to listen to Palmer tell about taking up serpents and speaking in tongues and baptism with the Holy Ghost and fire, like he knew a bunch of stuff I didn't. He was always bad to show off like that. Still is.

I concentrated on those new clothes. Three hours passed. My father did not show. A couple more. Still no John Calvin. Palmer and I ran out of tracts and sat on a bench outside the courthouse, watching the clock. When my folks finally showed up, we headed straight out of town, southbound. I knew Lazy Larry's was to the north. I was heartsick. "What about my new clothes?"

My father rebuked me for my vanity, said I was bound by worldly pride and that I needed deliverance. I was being selfish. He said, "It's my night to preach and I need time to seek the Lord and I'm already running late."

I accused him and my mother of fibbing to me, of deliberately waiting until it was too late to go to Lazy Larry's, of knowing that the Blue Law meant we couldn't buy clothes on Sunday, of conniving, of playing me like a two-dollar fiddle. What I got out of all of that was them being even madder at me than I was at them, if such a thing were possible. My mother told me to leave her out of it. Palmer looked out the window the whole time and didn't say anything.

When we got to the brush arbor my father went over behind Uncle John Wesley's truck to seek the Lord in prayer.

I suspected that Uncle John Wesley was

pleased to see that no more had shown up for his brother John Calvin's preaching than for his own. In fact, there was one fewer. Bob the egg man did not return.

At seven-thirty he asked Palmer—Palmer!—to open the service with prayer, which Palmer made the most of. "Father God," (I cannot sound like Palmer when he was ten, and wouldn't if I could. Imagine if a weasel could talk.) "Father God, I ask you to come into this great sanctuary and dwell among us. And I just ask you bless them that keeps your commandments and honors their father and mother, and convict and chastise them that does not. Honor their father and mother, I mean. Chastise 'em real hard. Praise Jesus. And this we ask in your mighty name."

I asked God if he really wanted to be associated with somebody like Palmer.

The song service, as usual, consisted entirely of hymns I could imagine Dracula singing. About halfway through *When I See the Blood* there was a rustle behind me, as the night before, but this one was accompanied by a wave of gaseous effluvium of a sort that could issue only from the diseased depths of a drunkard's belly. That and perfume. I did not have to sneak a look to see who it was.

After the offering, Uncle John Wesley gave my father a little introduction: "Brother John Calvin is the one preaching tonight, so let's just hold him up and ask the Lord to bless him with the anointing. Brother John Calvin?"

My father got up there in back of that olive drab pulpit, looked out over that multitude of twenty and said, "*For where two or three are gathered together in my name, there am I in the midst of them.*"

John Calvin Singleton could go from conversational to cataclysmic faster than any Pentecostal preacher I've ever heard. The "anointing," they called it. My father had the anointing that night. He and the Lord were all worked up about some stuff.

When he was preaching mad my father liked to start out in the Old Bible, heavy on the law, light on the love, before moving on to something nasty from the New Testament, usually from the Apostle Paul.

My father found me with his eyes and said, like there was nobody else there, "Ecclesiastes 11:10. '*Put away evil from thy flesh, for childhood and youth are vanity.*'"

He went on. "You don't have to be an adult to be carried away by vanity. The devil is a wonder. A lying wonder. He tells you, 'You're just a little bit smarter than everybody else, better looking, too. A sport like you oughta have some fancy clothes. You're too good for the ones you got.'

He turned to Palmer and said, "'*Children, obey your parents in everything, for this pleases the Lord.*' Amen?"

Palmer hollered, "Colossians, 3:20!"

My father said, "Praise Jesus! That's little Brother Palmer, there, John Wesley's boy."

Then he again fixed his steely stare straight at little Sam, reared back, and said, "Deuteronomy 9:24! *'Ye have been rebellious against the Lord from the day that I knew you,'*" and lit into the awfullest denunciation of rebellious youth you ever heard. Before he was done he had as much as thrown me in with beatniks and communists and folk singers. I knew that everybody else knew that he was talking about me.

He went on, "That spirit of rebellion leads you to question everything. But you already know it all, so can't nobody tell you nothing, neither. Ephesians 5:6 *'Because of these things cometh the wrath of God upon the children of disobedience.'* The wrath of God on the children of disobedience. Oh, you don't want to be standing there when God goes to pouring down wrath on the children of disobedience. Amen? You will not be thinking about how you are dressed when God starts pouring down wrath. 'Oh Mommy! Oh Daddy!' Sorry, son, it's too late to honor thy father and mother. It's too late to obey God. That boat done left the dock. Now comes the wrath. But, oh, sinner, backslider, you know who you are. God is speaking to your heart. He's saying, there's still time. There's still time tonight. There's still time for you to get down on your knees and repent and get back to the Lord. There is still time. But - don't - you - push - it.

"Now, Sister Ethylene, if you would play *The Blood Shall Never Lose Its Power*, I feel that the Lord is working on the heart of one who's been vain and rebellious against the Lord."

He switched to his altar call voice and went into the whole every eye closed bit. I knew that everybody else knew he expected me to come forward. I was not among that night's penitents.

Bernace was. She walked right up the saw-dust trail and knelt at the cross and believed in her heart and confessed with her mouth the Lord Christ Jesus and was saved on the spot, on the bottom of a Holy Roller dog pile—everybody praising God and otherwise raising their voices high unto the hills. It was as close to pandemonium as eighteen Pentecostals could manage.

I remained in my seat, cogitating the sermon, and, as was always the case when the Holy Ghost descended and tongues began to be spoken and people went to dancing in the spirit, wishing I were anywhere else on earth.

A big thick hand settled squarely on the top of my head. I could not have turned around even if I'd had the nerve to. Birch Blake himself, he and his breath, said, "You know this is all horse shit don't you, boy?" Then the hand was gone and so was Birch.

After a little, things began to settle down up front; Bernace was crying and everybody seemed happy. My father asked Aunt Ethylene to dismiss us in prayer.

I was still mad on Sunday. My father tried to make nice to me but I wasn't having any. My mother either. Right after I asked God the same question I asked every morning—why can't taters taste like bacon?—I went off to work on my sermon up behind the spring house. By two o'clock it was done. It practically came together on its own.

Anybody thinks I was too mature to use an opportunity like this to get back at my folks would be giving me too much credit. I stayed out of sight until the sun was just touching the tops of the western hills, till I figured everybody'd be getting antsy about making it to the revival on time. Then I waited just a little longer and moseyed casually down to the house. My father was standing on one foot then the other, about to have a spell.

"Where have you been?" The harshness in his voice came as music to my ears. "We're late and we were supposed to go over your message. I swear to my time, I ought to know better than to depend on any little boy. I wouldn't except for your mother. I flat told her." My mother slammed the car door. I got in the back seat, happy.

When we arrived, at seven-thirty-five, we had to hunt for a place to park. There must've been close to thirty cars. The brush arbor was packed and a lot of vehicles were pulled right up close so folks could sit on the hoods and fenders and still join in the doings.

My father looked annoyed and said, "Well, the fat's in the fire, now."

I said I needed time to seek the Lord in prayer. He couldn't say anything to that. So I went off behind Uncle John Wesley's truck where I spent a good five minutes not seeking the Lord in prayer. I finished up, and then took a seat on the platform, as Aunt Ethylene was finishing *Saved by the Blood*.

The meeting proceeded in the usual order, a couple of the strangers testified, a couple more made prayer requests. I could tell that the offering was a good one. I asked God to lead them to give some of it to me to buy some goddamn clothes with.

It was Uncle John Wesley introduced me. "This young man that's fixing to come up here and share the word as the spirit of God gives him utterance, was called to preach when he was just eight years old. Praise Jesus. *For a child shall lead them*, amen?" Big chorus of amens.

"This is little Sam Singleton, and he is so full of the Holy Ghost and fire he can't hardly shut up. Praise Jesus. Out of the mouths of babes. Instead of playing of a Saturday, he was over to Houston learning how to witness from my boy Palmer. He follows Palmer around asking him questions on the Word. And my Palmer, he is a born teacher. Praise Jesus. So I want y'all to just believe the

Lord that the anointing will take hold of young Sam Singleton! And bless him and bless us with what he's fixing to preach. Little Brother Sam."

I was going to offer up something complimentary about Uncle John Wesley till he made me sound like I was Palmer's protégé. So I just walked right to the pulpit, shiny corduroys and everything, and began.

Now, you'll have to imagine me with my little Brother Sam voice talking to the congregation there. I said, "Most of y'all were not here when both Uncle, I mean Brother John Wesley and Brother John Calvin started out their messages quoting Matthew 18:20, '*For where two or three are gathered together in my name, there am I in the midst of them.*' That verse gets quoted every time nobody shows up for church, like last night and Friday night.

"But that's not all there is to Matthew 18. There's this: "*At the same time came the disciples unto Jesus, saying, Who is the greatest in the kingdom of heaven? And Jesus called a little child unto him.*'

"And last night Brother John Calvin preached Ecclesiastes 11:10: '*Childhood and youth are vanity.*'

"And that gets me back to Matthew 18. This is Jesus talking. '*But whoso shall offend one of these little ones which believe in me, it were better for him that a millstone were hanged about his neck, and that he were drowned in the depth of the sea.'*

"But that's not what I'm fixing to preach on. It's just a little housekeeping. Tonight I'm taking as my text Luke 19, and this little book right here, which I'll get to directly.

"*'He,'*" that's Jesus, "*'sent two of his disciples, Saying go ye into the village— where ye shall find a colt tied, whereupon a man never set. Loose him and bring him hither. And if any man ask you why do you loose him, Thus shall ye say unto him, 'Because the Lord hath need of him.'*

"And just so you know, everybody seems to agree that this wasn't really a colt, so much as a donkey. These two donkey rustling disciples went to town, and were in the process of borrowing that donkey, without permission, when, sure enough, the rightful owners came up on 'em, red-handed, you might say, and asked where did they think they were going with that donkey. And the rustlers just kept right on with what they were doing and said unto the rightful owners, *'The Lord hath need of him.'*

"See, that is faith in action, right there. Most folks would flat decline, some guy in sandals tells them to commit grand theft donkey. The police chariot pulls you over and the cop asks to see some license and registration. You say, *'The Lord hath need of him?'* Maybe the donkey's owners hath need to press charges. The penitentiaries are full of guys who hath need for things. How is 'The Lord hath need of him' any different than when John Dillinger hath need of a bank's money? And you know what they call it when Willie Mays hath need of second base.

"'Thou shalt not steal.' That's the Eighth Commandment. Sounds simple but it isn't. Seems like even Jesus himself wasn't clear on it. And neither are some other folks I could name. The Ten Commandments may have been graven in stone, but for some people they might as well have been written in sand. Same with every other law, God's and man's.

"That donkey is one handy beast of burden. Thanks to him, all these centuries later, when some folks are on their way to work or church and broke and hath need of some free gas, they can just use the hose they keep in the trunk to siphon some out of a parked car.

And there are other donkey-related exceptions to the Eighth Commandment. There's one for when you hath need of roastin' ears, one for when you hath need of peach tree cuttings, one for when you hath need of lumber, one for when you hath need of a watermelon. And plenty of others, too.

"I've heard you can go to hell the same for lying as you can for stealing. But that's not so clear, either, for some folks. Where is the line between a little lie, which is OK—'Palmer, those high-water britches make you look taller'—and a big ugly lie straight outa the pit, like when you promise somebody something in order to get your way, then go back on your word?

"And when you never give back what you bor-
row, or pay what you owe? 'I'd druther owe it to
you forever than do you out of it,' is one way of
putting it. Is that stealing? Or is it lying?"

My father sprang from his chair behind me
and clamped his hand over my mouth, which
was unfortunate because I hadn't even gotten to
my book yet.

"Devil, I rebuke you! In the mighty name of
Jesus I command you to come out of this boy!"

Then they were all crowded around me. They
shoved me to the ground, forcing me to kneel
at the altar, and somebody anointed my head
with oil. Everybody was yelling and praying and
climbing all over me, breathing on me, putting
their sweaty hands on me. My father kept casting out devils, commanding them to come out of
there in the name of Jesus. Uncle John Wesley
had ahold of my arms, holding them straight up
by the wrists, and kept asking me if I accepted
Jesus's forgiveness. That if I would but humble
myself he would come into my wicked heart and
give me succor. I didn't like the sound of that.

Through a space in all the knees and butts, I
could make out Birch. He was standing between
two cars, and looking straight at me.

I prayed along until at last the grown-ups
were satisfied that I had been redeemed and allowed me to stand. I looked outside and Birch
was gone.

If God had forgiven me, John Calvin and Maureen Sedgwick Singleton were less kindly disposed. They commanded me to prepare an apology, especially to them and the rest of the family, which I was to write out and read aloud before I went to bed, then deliver from the pulpit the next night. I wrote it. And I was ashamed of myself for not defying them. But, as I say, I was nine.

Naturally, the ten minute drive up to the brush arbor on Monday evening seemed to take forever. Deep morbid dread, that's what it was.

We got to Birch's and there was no brush arbor. It was gone. Actually, it had simply returned to its former state, was once more a common pile of trash. It looked as if a big thick hand had come straight out of the sky and flattened it, except for the upright piano, which stood proud, shrouded in debris, like the fireplace of a tornado-struck farm house.

Birch was parked on his stump, can in hand. He said, "I told you one week."

My father looked like he might start something, but settled for saying, "A week? We've only had three meetings. Friday, Saturday, and Sunday. That is flat not a week."

Birch still did not stand, didn't even raise his voice. He said, "John Calvin, you stood right here last Monday, one week ago to the day, and agreed when I told you you had one week. Don't say you didn't cause you did. One week. Now get that shit off my place. And I don't mean when you can get to it."

When Uncle John Wesley arrived we loaded the remains back onto the flatbed truck, and hauled them off to be dumped on the side of County Road PP, where, so far I know, they remain to this day. Aunt Winnie and Palmer posted themselves down by the road to tell the ones who showed up that the meeting had been cancelled due to an act of— Well, it was definitely not an act of God.

We moved out of Tick Holler a week later, on my tenth birthday, in the middle of the night, up to St. Joe, and had been there a little less than a month when Aunt Winnie called and asked if the big explosion down in Texas County had made the news up our way. Birch Blake's brand new forty-seven-radiator industrial still blew up the first time he ran it.

"They say he got third degree burns over seventy-five percent of his body."

She called back the next day and said Birch died at the hospital up in Jeff City. According to my father he went to hell.

I wrote a question in my book: "You know this is all horseshit, don't you, boy?"

... a participatory theater piece, presented here without the audience.

The Singleton Bible

Brother Sam's Testimony

An Appreciation of Appreciation

The Singleton Bible

And everybody said Goddamn. I'm sure that it has occurred to most everybody here that if the average believer knew the Bible as well as the average atheist, there'd be more atheists and fewer believers. Which brings us to Brother Sam's bible class. Today's lesson is from the Singleton Bible, not one passage, the entire thing, which is notable for its brevity, being Brother Sam's take on the King James Version. Clear away the repetition and bibledygook and all the main points fit on a sheet of letter paper.

The Bible takes place a long time ago and is set in Heaven, Hell, and the Eastern Mediterranean area of Earth. Heaven is described as having many mansions, streets of gold, and pearly gates—a place of opulent trashiness. Live a virtuous life and you wind up having to move in with Donald Trump. Very little of the action takes place in Heaven.

Even less of the action takes place in Hell,

which seems to have served as the model for the modern subway. It is a place deep underground where it's hot, crowded, and noisy, and everybody is mean. Like Heaven, Hell does not exist in any sense other than the imaginary.

In fact, the entire Bible is enacted within an area smaller than Texas. It would've been a somewhat different book had it been set in Texas. And it is easy to imagine God being from Texas. The governor of Texas.

The Bible is lousy with characters, but only a few of 'em bear mention. You've probably heard of **God**. He makes himself. And everything else. But is just dumber'n a stump and meaner'n cat dirt. I'd hate to think what the universe would look like if his creativity hadn't petered out after only six days.

God (the Father), **Jesus** (the Son) and the **Holy Ghost** comprise the three prongs of the Trinity but claim to be the same guy, which must drive the census takers crazy. I personally would find it uncomfortable having my own ghost around while I was s'til alive, but that's the way God prefers it.

He is his own son, too.

Simon says, "So, uh, Jesus, if you're your own father, then you must've slept with your mother."

"No," says Jesus, "that was the Holy Ghost prong."

Satan is the fourth prong of the trinity, you

might say. His function is mainly decorative—to provide a contrast flattering to God. Satan is also handy for blaming stuff on, even though God is, of course, entirely responsible for everything. Satan is the grown-up. God is the spoiled child. Satan is God's moral superior to the extent that Satan never once made anybody do anything unpleasant to a penis. On the goddamn contrary. God makes Hell for Satan to live in, which suits Satan just fine, just so God is not there, which, being omnipresent, he is. Goddamn. God could learn a lot from Satan but is insufficiently self-aware.

God makes **Adam** and **Eve** but naturally fucks up the job. And when their interests extend beyond gardening, he goes into a snit and evicts them from their home. Some time thereafter, God gets to be so distraught with his own boundless ineptitude that he has one of his periodic breakdowns and just drowns everything on earth except one family and their pets. You can see why God has more aliases than Whitey Bulger.

"Aren't you the one that drowned all those people?"

"No. I'm Jehovah. That was Yahweh."

Abraham is the archetype of the terrible father. He also starts the circumcision craze notwithstanding the state of cutlery during the early Bronze Age.

Moses claims that God has given him ten

laws, or thereabouts, all of which carry the death penalty. Most of them serve only to aggrandize God. Three simply formalize what people already accept as necessary to living in communities: no killing, no stealing, no telling lies on somebody else.

David demonstrates the efficacy of projectiles as weapons by killing a more powerful foe from a safe distance. Founds the National Rock Association.

The **Old Testament** is the story of humankind's attempts to live with God's mistakes.

The first part of the **New Testament** is mainly about the Son prong of the Trinity, Jesus, who, like other members of his gang, operates under a number of street names: Horn of Salvation, Merciful Redeemer, J.F. Christ. Any carpenter who winds up with nails driven clean through both hands and both feet probably should think about some other line of work. He does attain a level of immortality, in spite of his failure to make a go of an honest trade like carpentry. I can only hope that two thousand years in the future when people smash their thumb they shout "Sam Fucking Singleton!"

The second part of the New Testament is mainly about **Paul**, who creates Christianity in his own misogynistic, homophobic, anti-Semitic, paranoid image, and ordains himself the world's first evangelist. The thirteen books of the New Testament for which Paul claims credit set forth the prejudices and hatreds that define Christianity to this day.

Revelation reveals the primitive state of the fantasy fiction genre in the second century. You might as well read L. Ron Hubbard's Dianetics.

You can pore over in the minutest detail the two testaments, and parse their events and analyze their characters 'til Hell won't have it, but to reveal the totality of the Bible's eternal truth—you must look between the lines. And there is nothing whatsoever between the lines. Empty space. Blank. Devoid of content. Goddamn.

Brother Sam's Testimony

Preaching was my family's trade, or would've been if any of us coulda made a living off of it. As it was, it was a calling, which is like a trade, only you do not need to know anything or be able to do anything. You don't need skill; you just need almighty gall. Go to any church and see for yourself.

Almost four years, that's how long I was out on the sawdust trail as a child evangelist, and my family's main bread winner. Our base of operations changed six times. I changed, too. Sometime not long after my twelfth birthday I refused to preach anymore. I told my folks that God had withdrawn the call. They tried to argue, but I knew I had 'em. I said God had something else in mind for me which he would divulge when the time was right. I'd let them know as soon as the word came down. Thus began my two year walk to the door.

I knew that whatever truth was, my people were strangers to it. I knew that their religion was wrong in both senses of the word: it was false and it was immoral.

In my retirement I set about investigating other religions. I figured Judaism was more authentic than Christianity, but Judaism, and Islam, too, forbade the very foodstuffs I'd never got enough of. Bacon now, versus paradise at some point in the future, is what I'd call a classic bird-in-the-hand deal. Give me the pork, thank you. At least I stopped short of Jehovah's Witnessism and Mormonism. I was curious, not crazy.

Bidding fare thee well to the Abrahamic religions, I wanted to see if some entirely different tradition might work out better. The local Buddhists met in the back room of a furniture store, like Holy Rollers might. And their congregation was small, too— maybe twenty. Nice folks. But I found it absurd to think that all suffering comes from desire. Buddha started out a rich prince; he was poor on purpose. Not the example I was looking for. And just so you know, desire fuels civilization. I know it fuels Brother Sam. Goddamn.

Hinduism advocates the caste system. No fair. Besides, reincarnation is just as preposterous as heaven and hell.

Even as I was turning over every flat rock for a religion that made sense, I was wising up. So, with each one, it got to be a harder sell. I made up this list of the sects I checked into between the ages of twelve and fourteen:

Baptist, Methodist,
  Four Square, Nazarene,
Lutheran, Hugonot,
  Animist, Tridentine,
Sadducee, Orthodox,
  Philistine, Oriental,
Essene, Augustine,
  Pharisee, Transcendental,
Babism, Calvinism,
  Hinduism, Santeria,
Basilidian, Tondrakian,
  Simonian, Episcopalian,
Levite, Hutterite,
  Ophrite, Ananda Marga,
Mennonite, Cainite,
  Russelite, Siddharta,
Latter Day, Seventh Day,
  Bible Way, Rosecrutian,
Islam, Gideon,
  Anglican, Hare Krishna,
Caodaism, Legalism,
  Satanism, Coptic,
Jainism, Judaism,
  Cynicism, Gnostic,
Puritan, Pagan,
  Hedonist, Chiropractic,
Shaker, Quaker,
  Manichean, Anabaptist,
Wiccan, Davidian,
  Pithian, Homeopathic,
Druid, Hoo Doo,

Sam Singleton, Atheist Evangelist

Voo Doo, Apostolic,
Adventist, Demonic,
  Histrionic, Catatonic,
Davite, Elkasite,
  Borborite, Dunkard,
Kabala, Ebionite,
  Anonymous Drunkard,
Platonism, Shinto,
  Aztec Noggin Ball,
Hubbardite, Church of God,
  Church of Satan, Holy Roller,
Unitary, Presbytery,
  Rasta Faerie, Pasta Fairy,
Church of Christ, Church of Jesus,
  Church of Doing what You Pleases.

And that does not include the really strange
ones. I read the Bible, which is pretty strange,
from start to finish when I was fourteen, more or
less to see if I'd missed anything. Before I got to
the end I was an atheist. I did not think it best to
let my folks in on the good news just yet.

We were living in Houston—not the one in
Texas County, Missouri, or the one in Arkansas,
or even the one in Mississippi, the one in Texas—
and I was in the ninth grade. Morris Cerullo, a
big-time evangelist, put on a revival at the Music
Hall. They made me go.

Brother Cerullo told about growing up in
a Jewish orphanage, and how, when he was
fourteen, he had a personal visitation from Jesus.
You see, Jesus recognized little Morris's criminal

potential. Jesus is like a talent scout for the mob. He told Morris that he could be a millionaire evangelist, but, naturally, he'd have to convert. Jesus explained that one Jew was about all Holy Rollers could abide, and he had dibs. The first thing the Apostle Paul did when he invented evangelism was to stop calling himself a Jew and start calling himself a Christian. So that was the way it was done, which was OK with Morris.

Affiliation aside, being an evangelist naturally entails being a showoff. Morris Cerullo laid over 'em all. When he wrapped up his sermon about himself, he commanded everybody between the ages of twelve and twenty to come up on stage. I had to go up there with the others. There were hundreds of us. The supporting pastors, who had been sitting on stage, formed us into rows.

Brother Cerullo says, "The power of God will lay these young people out like a platter of frozen fish sticks!"

It was common for people at revivals to be "slain in the spirit." *Singleton's Holy Roller Handbook and Field Guide* defines that as pretending to pass out. Usually it'd be limited to a few people, always up front where there happened to be room for 'em to sprawl. The Holy Ghost was considerate like that. Brother Cerullo was gonna demonstrate slaying in the spirit on an industrial scale.

He reaches out and taps this boy on the

forehead, and goddamn if the boy doesn't fall backward like he's been shot. A couple of the pastors ease him to the floor. Then Brother Cerullo does the same thing to the next one in line. And the next one. I'm back in about row eight. And he's coming my way fast. I am debating whether I am gonna pretend to be slain the spirit, or face the fallout. I do not want Brother Cerullo, or the thousands of people in the hall, to mistake me for a chump. But there I am. And Brother Cerullo is laying out the teenagers, one by one.

And then he's standing right in front of me. Up close he's this sweaty little pink-faced guy with a dye job, reeeking of Aqua Velva. He looks at me, without looking at me, and says into the microphone, "The Holy Ghost has something special in store for this young man," and floats that hand out there and raps me just a lick on the brow. I'm still computing the consequences of not playing along. Will he rear back and give 'er another poke? Will he have two or three pastors take me aside and offer to kick my hippie ass if I don't get with the goddamn program? No. I know exactly what he'll do. He'll ask the entire congregation to join him in praying me through to salvation on the spot. So I settle for giving him a sharp look, to convey how I know this is all horseshit, and then rock back on my heels like a fucking idiot.

So now I'm lying there on the stage of the Music Hall and around me hundreds of youngsters are all pretending to be unconscious. The crowd is shouting and speaking in tongues. It sounds like all hell, and looks like the final dress rehearsal for Jonestown, which, so far as I can say, Morris Cerullo had nothing to do with. I'm wondering how long I am gonna have to lie there. There is no way I'm gonna be the first one up. Or the last.

After a goddamned eternity, two or three minutes in clock time, movement overtook the deck around me, and the supine teenagers began to rise like reanimated corpses at the Second Coming.

It was sufficient time for a genesis to occur. Out of the dust of being lied to, being misled, being made a fool of, being shown off, being scared and miserable and hopeless, was created Sam Singleton, Atheist Evangelist. I arose, and left that stage transformed, prepared to face the future on terms of my own choosing. I knew that my life was fixing to take a sharp turn toward the shitty. And I never felt better. Goddamn.

As for Morris Cerullo, I do not know if he has ever claimed the credit that is his due for the role he played in unleashing Sam Singleton, Atheist Evangelist on the world.

Well, that's my testimony.

An Appreciation of Appreciation

Goddamn. The title of this message I am about to deliver is *An Appreciation of Appreciation*. The word "thanks" appears in the King James Version of the Bible exactly one-hundred times. Ninety-nine of 'em are directed at God. Here's the sole exception. It's from the Apostle Paul, there in the sixteenth chapter of his epistle to the Romans. "Greet Priscilla and Aquila my helpers in Christ Jesus, who have for my life laid down their own necks: unto whom not only I give thanks, but also all the churches of the Gentiles." One thing about the Apostle Paul: he thought a great deal of himself. But he did give the world Christianity. So there's that. Goddamn Paul.

Anyway, that's the one time in the whole damned Bible in which anybody other than God gets any thanks and it's second-hand and they have to split it two ways. Not once in the Old Testament does anybody offer so much as a passing "'ppreciate it" to one of their fellow humans.

The King James Bible—and, lo, any other kind is just a little ol' toy bible, a Fisher-Price bible—the King James Version of the Bible is regarded as one of the greatest works of literature in the English canon. It's certainly one of the longest. This is the mythological history that subsequent dominant cultures the world over have claimed as their own— and only once in the Bible does one single person say thank you to another. No wonder everybody was mad all the time, running around, starting shit, slaying and smiting so.

Even though they were despicably rude to one another, they were polite as all get-out to their deity. With the deity it was, "Oh thank you! Thank you God! Seriously, God, we just thank the shit out of you."

And they imbued their deity with all their own worst qualities, so they could say that being morally, intellectually and emotionally weak was divine. Their god was racist and sexist and homophobic and generally ignorant and intolerant. Absolutely self-interested. Naturally, they made it a boy deity.

And he was above all, as Brother Sam is wont to point out, wildly mad with jealousy. Along those same lines, he was insecure and covetous. And chief among all the things their god coveted, all the things he hogged, was gratitude. He insisted that every damned bit of credit and praise go to himself. Like I say, the people created him, so they got to make him crazy like that. They said they were created in his image. And they used the deity being a fucking creep as a pretext for their own despicable rudeness.

Like this Jesus character. He combined the worst attributes of God and man.

One time he's visiting with this Pharisee by the name of Simon (the Bible is thick with guys named Simon). And while Jesus is talking to Simon there, this harlot (these days we say sex worker) walks in off the street and gets down at Jesus's feet and starts in to crying and literally washing his feet with her tears. Apparently the mere sight of the Lord's aching feet set her off like that. You may have heard the story. And she rubs ointment on his crusty-assed first century feet then wipes them with her hair. And the whole time she's just smothering those smelly old dogs with kisses right there on the floor in front of all these winebibbers and publicans and lawyers.

Simon is a bit of a Puritan. He says to himself, but so Jesus can't help overhearing, he says: "Verily. Man of God oughtn't to be consorting with workers in the sex trade. Don't look right."

Jesus says, "Verily yourself, Simon. I don't see you ministering to my corns and calluses. Plus, I am setting an example here for subsequent generations of preachers regarding how they should deal with their sex workers; namely, wait till they finish pleasuring you, then forgive 'em for it. And you, little girl," for he spaketh to Martha, "you can just consider all your sins up to this point absolved. You missed a spot on my heel there."

And Simon mumbles something like, "Sure I want to go to heaven, but I don't know about this foot thing. Goddamn."

The moral is: It does not matter what you do. Seriously. You can get down on the floor and wash Jesus's feet with your fucking tears. Your tears for Christ's sake. And kiss those feet and slather 'em with unguent and get 'em all up in your hair. And there is no way any part of the godhead is gonna say thanks. He may offer to forgive your sins or some equally meaningless shit, but don't look for a simple "Thank you for the toe job." And forget about a tip.

Nobody in the Bible, certainly not Jesus, knows anything about the simple satisfaction that comes from offering a sincere thank you to one who deserves it. Nothing of being on the receiving end of that worthy thanks. Their loss. You'd feel sorry for 'em if they weren't such assholes.

And beyond the humane impetus to say thank you, common courtesy enables folks to live co-operatively around each other. Like I say, to see what happens in the absence of good manners, read the Bible. Everything goes to hell. Can't no-body get along. Somebody say goddamn.

Gratitude is among the more becoming of

human attributes. Its absence is seen, or felt, as acutely uncivilized. Anybody who withholds the thanks you got coming is a jerk. But way worse than that is delivering that thanks to the wrong party. That'll flat torque your nut. It is an offense against fairness.

Who would be such a lowdown, no-con-science-having, cretinous carton of crap as to do anybody that way?

Let me illustrate. On my way here, Friday, I just come-a-one of getting caught up in a five car wreck on I-5. It was awful. They had the inter-state closed both ways. A man died. Folks were badly injured. And if I'd happened along just a minute or two earlier I could've been right in the middle of that. And I am thankful I wasn't. Something (actually, it was my bladder, is what it was) made me choose that exact time to stop and do as nature intends. So, even as the carnage was being cleared, there I was, safely stuck in the traffic jam, basking in the afterglow of bodily re-lief cherished by all travelers.

Of course, my making a pit stop right in time to avoid the wreck was just a coincidence. If I were still a believer I'd be bound to ascribe that timely urge to purge to the creator of the uni-verse working his divine purpose by means of my urinary tract.

So, while I was sitting there, I got to thinking how many of the people in those other cars and trucks, all backed up for miles in both directions, were thanking God for their deliverance from calamity. Not me, of course. I mean, I was thankful. I have no problem using thankful and appreciative and grateful and glad to describe my feelings when circumstances break my way, when chance happens to favor my interests.

I found myself pondering who would I thank if I took a mind to credit somebody for my being spared, even though they had nothing to do with it. And I decided that the next time I saw Sister Jones I would thank her. Sister Jones? Stand up, please. I want to thank you for doing that thing you did with my bladder so I did not become just one more atheist evangelist-shaped stain on the pavement. Now let's everybody just raise our voices in praise to Sister Jones. Praise Sister Jones! Goddamn.

Oh! I heard somebody say, "Brother Sam, but Sister Jones is not God." That is exactly right. Sister Jones exists. See? Look at 'er. And me thanking her certainly makes no less sense than those other people thanking God. Giving God the credit for that coincidence doesn't screw Sister Jones out of her due.

But when believers divert the stream of praise that common decency reserves for the worthy, for the nourishment of the individual and the community, I am obliged to call bullshit on 'em.

It wouldn't be in the least surprising if one of the injured out there on the highway, having been saved by the combined efforts of EMTs and nurses and physicians, gave the credit to their deranged deity. "Suck eggs, trauma team. I'm thanking God."

Now, if I were one of those medical professionals I would want to say something my damn self, along the lines of, "Next time haul your dying ass to church, you fucking ingrate. What do you want with some old medical professional? Get Jesus on the mainline. Tell him what you want." Goddamn.

Even the perfunctory thanks offered by a fast-food server has value. It honors cooperation, the very basis of society. It is directed *to* somebody. What if the person who handed you your Happy Meal, and took your money, looked skyward and thanked Jesus? I am not a man to advocate throwing food, but I couldn't say you nay if you heaved a French fry at 'em.

Don't blame God for the bad behavior of the godly. What with not existing, God does not have the power to co-opt the measure of gratitude that you or I have coming. That bit of ethical skullduggery takes a human actor. And what a rotten business it is. It cheapens the very idea of sincere gratitude, rendering it so inconsequential as to be blithely bestowed on some hoo doo. For shame. Antisocial-behavior-wise, I'm not sure which is worse, thanking the wrong party or thanking an imaginary party. I guess that's the difference between bad and crazy.

Either way, for theists nothing on earth can ever be truly first-rate— and that's crazy. Turning up your nose at what this life offers, in the pursuit of a bigger payoff in some additional life, does not make you holy. It makes you a jackass. A holy jackass. And a greedy jackass. So you'll fit right in in heaven.

Which gets us back to God cornering the market on gratitude. Of the billions of times some human has offered deeply felt thanks, God has never acknowledged it, even once. And if I were that hypothetical believer, and I were hoping God might sometime speak to me like he does to presidential candidates, the very first words out of God's mouth had better be "You're welcome," or, "Don't mention it." That'd be acceptable. Anything else? I'd tell him to go to Hell. And I don't mean Michigan.

Goddamn.

CATS SHEEP AND GOATS

The Taxonomy of Atheists, Believers, and Preachers

Goddamn. I was having a beer with a few friends and we got to talking about when and whether to debate the existence of God with believers, something I myself will not do. I reckon how the question of ghosts, goblins, and invisible monsters has long been settled to the satisfaction of any adult with any sense. Which does not include my cousin Palmer, with whom I grew up and remain close. Don't ask me why I make an exception for Palmer; I do not know, aside from the fact that he is the only Singleton who'll still have anything to do with me. I no longer expect to bring him around, and he knows perfectly well that his chances of convincing me to go back to believing in God are nil.

Let me tell you a little about Palmer. He attended Oral Roberts University. I know that Oral is no longer around to defend himself, but, if he were, I would tell him to his face; anybody whose full name is Granville Oral Roberts and goes by his middle name is either bragging or advertising. Which I can appreciate. The Robertses have always been good with their mouths, going all the way back to Great-Grandpa B.J.

Palmer laid out good money for a so-called degree in theological-historical studies, which you have to be an ORU grad to say with a straight face. I told Palmer that he should've gone to barber college so he'd have a legit trade, unlike any other Singleton male for as far back as anybody can say. And he would have done it, too, if he coulda got past the entrance exam. So now he works at the Coca Cola call center there in Tulsa, counseling people about their soda pop issues. He told me he got written up for witnessing to callers. I told him he better lay off warning folks about hell and stick to warning 'em about Pepsi. In fact, the decent thing would be to encourage 'em to switch to beer. He won't. So far as I can say, Palmer has never even tried beer. Or wine.

When holy rollers take comunion, they use grape juice. No kidding. Drinking, even sacramental drinking, is a sin. And Jesus could not commit a sin. Ergo, Jesus made grape juice, not wine. Grape juice, for Christ's sake. Well that's no crazier than Catholics claiming that the communion wine and host become the actual blood and tissue of Jesus. Jesus was not specific about what part of him the tissue sample comes from.

Palmer says Catholics have got it all wrong about transubstantiation, that you have to know when the Bible is being literal and when it's not.

I asked Palmer how he knows which is which. He said through "spiritual discernment." The Holy Ghost reveals it to him. Well, I said to Palmer, I said, "You lie to your friends and I'll lie to mine, but let's not lie to each other."

So now he's mad at me. I am torn between believing in Palmer's potential, and doubting that he will ever live up to it. Admitting you've been a schmuck your entire life takes character. And the likelihood, hell, the dead sure certainty, of being shunned by the ones you love is not for the faint of heart.

Palmer would be a preacher like Brother Sam—well, not like Brother Sam, but a preacher—if he could tolerate speaking in front of a group. But he cannot keep his voice from quivering. He'll stand up and testify at church, but that's about all the public speaking Palmer can abide. Even then it's like his internal amplifier is set to tremolo. Plus, Palmer's voice never changed from when he was a child. Mine neither. I sounded just like this when I was five. Anyway, Palmer is not endowed with what you might call natural vocal gifts. Which is odd, because the Singletons are known as loud talkers. Having a squeaky voice is not necessarily a bar to a career in hornswoggling. Plenty of preachers have annoying voices. But a big part of getting across as a preacher is the ability to scare people. Palmer couldn't scare a fly off a gut wagon. Of course, the fly might fall off the gut wagon laughing at the way Palmer sounds. And, just so you know, I do not hold with poking fun at peoples' physical attributes. And I do not count Palmer's voice against him.

What I object to is that Palmer is like most other superstitious twits. Anytime he feels the need to make a case for the existence of God, he invokes science. The rest of the time he has no use whatsoever for science. And science is among the many subjects about which Palmer knoweth not his shit from his Shine-Ola. And for which he has nothing but contempt 'til he or one of his loved-ones needs a doctor, then he's perfectly happy to let science pick up where God leaves off. Not the other way around. When he and I are tussling over this god deal, he's all the time trying to burnish his own base superstition with the warm luster of scientific fact. I am no scientist, but I can rule out God or Isis or Santa without pretending to know more than I do.

Palmer is incurious to the point of block-headedness. Somebody told him that curiosity killed the cat, and he took it to heart. Which he needn't have, seeing as how the animal he resembles most is a sheep.

Still, he thinks he's gonna show me up by citing various august scientific sources. Palmer, or any other believer, using science to defend superstition is like putting a sun bonnet on a pile of shit. They happily avail themselves of science's benefits and protections in everyday life then

turn around and deny its most essential prin-
ciples, impede its progress, and disparage its
practitioners.

Anyway, Palmer called me, the other evening, and we got to contending over the usual
shit, 'til finally I told him, I said, "Palmer, I hate
to think where you and I would be today if y'all
believers had got your way at key points over the
past couple or three millennia. What if, for instance, y'all had succeeded in thwarting all the
advances in medical science that underlie the
care everybody—believers included—now take
for granted? What if believers had managed to
negate the very idea of the circulation of blood?
The cell. The germ theory. You know the answer,
Palmer, dying at age thirty and goddamn glad of
it, what with the brutishness and disease and un-
treatable injuries and all. You won't admit it, but
you're glad that reason and science have won,
and that the godly have lost, as often as they have
down through history. I told him, You know another thing believers get wrong? This shit about
there not being any atheists in foxholes. There
are no Biblical literalists in foxholes. Say there's
a soldier —a Christian soldier—all hunkered in a
foxhole, and a mortar round blows his arm half
off. Is the first word out of his mouth "Medic!" or
"Chaplain!" Goddamn.

Then this morning Palmer called me on the
phone again. He was just shitting roman candles
about something Brother Sam said or wrote. I do

not understand why Palmer persists in keeping tabs on samsingleton dot com but he does and it always makes him mad so he has to call up and harsh out on me for maltreating God.

So I said to Palmer, I said, "You're sticking up for God because he can't stick up for himself. Under most circumstances that would be admirable. Now, if you were talking about a child or somebody's who's old or infirm or mentally disabled, I'd admire the shit out of your willingness to speak up on their behalf. But you're telling me that this is the most powerful being in the entire universe and he needs you to defend him. I mean, as mere humans go, I suppose you're as good as the next one, but how do you think that looks to God? I think your average omnipotent being is gonna say, "Who needs you, you presumptuous little pissant. I need looking after, I'll do it my damn self." That's what he's gonna say. Or he'd say if he existed. Which he doesn't. And that's why he can't stick up for himself. So you feel the need to stick up for somebody, the woods are full of folks getting pushed around. They can use a champion. You want to take on that job, I'll stick up for you."

And as usual, Palmer just said he'd pray for me. Goddamn. His heart's in the right place, but his head's stuck up his ass. He accuses *me* of refusing to listen to reason.

I told Palmer, "If I'd listened to you and all the rest of the family, I would never have discovered beer, which has added way more meaning to my existence than God ever did. And if early humans had believed drinking beer was a sin, like y'all told me it was, where would humankind be, seeing as how beer was responsible for the rise of civilization? If I'd listened to y'all I would never have learned, through experience, that so many of the things I'd been warned against were not that bad. I'd also have failed to acquire certain lessons regarding consequences, in the here and now, not in the by and by, valuable and hard-won lessons. I would never have known how much of what I'd been told was bullshit. I wouldn't value the truth any more than fiction, not knowing which was which, assuming that all I'd been told was uniformly unreliable. Which it may not have been. Some of the stuff I got from my god-fearing family might've been good, though I cannot think of any off the top of my head.

"If I had listened to y'all I would have been denied the rich catharsis of cussing when cussing is called for, denied an entire vocabulary of some of the most powerful terms in the language." Goddamn. "If I'd listened to you I'd be in the position you're in now, Palmer, of not knowing what I'm talking about. You know nothing of being an atheist. I know exactly what it's like to be a believer."

The worst Palmer can say is that atheism is just another religion, which amounts to "Y'all are just as bad as we are." Imagine being accused of hypocrisy by a Christian. One shudders. I told Palmer, "When you say atheism is just another religion, you are wrong, at least as the word religion is commonly understood. I approve of the pejorative taint that that usage connotes. But it is a lie from the pit to say that atheism is a religion in the sense you reserve for your own belief, when you know it is not."

The Believing Class would prefer that there were no atheists, which could be accomplished in either of two ways. They could kill us or convert us. Pray let us consider only the second possibility. Conversion could happen in any of three ways: through coercion, through persuasion, or through redefinition. Coercion won't work. If the inconveniences and indignities already piled on atheists have failed to bring us to heel, no amount of additional bullying is likely to succeed. Persuasion is never gonna happen without evidence. But semantic slight of hand is cleaner than killing us and avoids having to convince us. How's this: you and your fellow believers accord to atheism the societal benefits heretofore reserved for a religion, and you can call us anything you like.

Palmer gets mad and starts talking about how he can't believe how much I hate God. If there's one thing Brother Sam hates it's being accused of hating, especially by the likes of Palmer. I love the guy, but goddamn.

This is not the first time somebody has

besmirched my name by associating it with hatred, not only of God, but of the godly.

If I had to defend myself every time Palmer or one of his credulous cohorts said something silly about me, I wouldn't have time for my main hobby, philately. Or any kind of sex. Just for Palmer's benefit I went on record about the scurrilous slander that Brother Sam hates God or the ones that say they believe in him. I don't hate believers because that would be wrong. I don't hate God because that would be stupid. Of course, if God existed, anybody with any sense, or a shred of decency, would have to, if not hate him, not exactly want him to marry into the family. Hating is never more a pathetic waste of time and energy than when the object of hatred exits only in the imagination. I can't hate God any more than believers can love him. I do despise the idea of God, much as believers love the idea of God. And, yes, I have been known to talk about being mad at God.

One of these times I'm gonna have to preach on irony. Brother Sam understands that an appreciation of irony is a lot to expect of some folks. The believers that accuse Brother Sam of hating God appear to be ironically impaired, so that their brains compensate by developing a fantastically heightened sense of hate. And they project their own hate on everybody else.

But I'll give Palmer and my holy roller kin and their pals credit for one thing: can't nobody hate like they can hate. Which is one of the reasons I had to claw my way out of the deep dark hole of bigotry and intolerance I was born into. The same hole Palmer still calls home. Too much hate.

I do wonder why, out of all the world's fictional or historical characters, or anybody he could stir up in his own imagination, Palmer latched onto this particular made-up play pal. I asked him why he didn't just pick Vlad the Impaler or Simon Legree. Couldn't he think of anybody nice? How about Pecos Bill? I told him, "Now there's a fantasy friend worth having. We used to read about Pecos Bill when were little."

I reminded Palmer about how Pecos Bill lassoed the tornado that dug out the Grand Canyon. Palmer says the Grand Canyon is only six thousand years old. And God put all those fossils and layers of rock in there to baffle scientists. Well, *The Saga of Pecos Bill* is a hell of a lot better yarn than that. And certainly no less plausible.

As for what Palmer and his pals down to the Blood of the Lamb Pentecostal Assembly and Full Gospel Family Worship Center accuse Brother Sam of? I do not care what they think. Plus, fuck 'em.

Palmer and I were both of us born into holy rolling, or Pentecostalism— same thing. If it were hereditary, I would be a carrier just like Palmer is. It is integral to my personality and my character. Even now I am cast in opposition to holy rolling.

And I am fine with that. Some atheists dislike the term "atheist" itself on account of how it defines us in terms of what we oppose. Not me. Abolitionists were defined in terms of what they opposed and you didn't hear them griping about it. And just because I outgrew holy rolling, doesn't alter the fact that I was imbued from birth with holy roller values. Listened to holy roller talk and holy roller music. Acquired holy roller loves and hates, holy roller folkways, the holy roller manner of speaking. My siblings, cousins, and childhood playmates were little holy rollers. My first girlfriends were holy rollers. I ran away at the age of twelve, with a holy roller evangelist. Then I ran away from the evangelist. With a holy roller biker gang, whom, oddly, did not call themselves the Holy Rollers. So, even when I went astray, I rolled right into a new hole. I say hole, but it was actually just another of countless depressions at the bottom of a great fetid pit so deep and so full of horseshit as to all but obscure any glimmer of sunlight. It took me 'til I was fourteen to gain the surface. I lost a lot of loved-ones in the process. But not Palmer. Palmer is faithful.

One well known professional atheist has equated a religious upbringing with child abuse. I don't know what you'd call Brother Sam's upbringing if not abuse, although the ones responsible for the snake-handling, tongues-speaking, and rest of the horrifying stuff that made a sick fucking nightmare of my childhood, didn't and still don't, see it that way.

Call it *training up a child in the way he should go*, per Proverbs 22:6, or casting him into the aforementioned fetid pit, it comes down to the same thing. Depending on your definition, it may not qualify as abuse, but it sure is near about the dirtiest trick a grown-up can play on a trusting child, a series of deceits guaranteed to put the child at a disadvantage when contending with real life. The first lie is that that disadvantage is offset by various benefits of membership in the Believing Class. And while it's true that they are many, and include some nice shit, like full participation and representation in the political process, those benefits come at the cost of the child's potential for unlimited discovery.

Palmer and his wife Cynthia Mae brought their children up as holy rollers. All but one of 'em, Ida Lee, the youngest girl and the pick of the litter, go to the same big ol' giant-ass holy roller bemusement park out there on the outskirts of Tulsa. They're already victimizing the next generation. Ida Lee went astray. She wound up at MIT with a PhD. in A.I. Artificial Intelligence. That's what Palmer displays when he talks about science. Artificial intelligence. Ida Lee is an atheist. Palmer doesn't know whether to be proud of her or ashamed of her.

Raising up children to believe in mythical beings may not have been abusive in ancient Thebes some fucking place, back when myths had to stand in for science by way of explaining the universe. I believe that sometime, not too long after Galileo and Copernicus, it became wrong to continue to teach children that it was factual when Joshua said, "The sun stood still in the midst of heaven and did not hasten to go down for about a whole day," or for that matter, that the sun was dragged across the sky every day by Helios in his little chariot. You know better. Don't play your children for chumps. What'd they ever do to you? Other than totally fuck up your life for all time.

Anyway, if you're a believer, and a parent, and of a mind to play some low down dirty shit on your offspring, teach them to accept the supernatural without evidence. Teach 'em that faith beats reason. That they can count on God to come through. That prayer can move mountains. And cure acne. Teach them that if they believe hard enough in something it will become so. Teach them to limit their aspirations and to accept their limitations. Convince those youngsters that they can only be so smart or so good. That it's OK to distrust and oppress and exclude anybody who doesn't accept their God. Tell 'em about how God is on their side. And that without God there can be no morality. See can you get 'em to believing that this life is a rehearsal for the real one that starts when they die. Instill in them godly selfishness of the sort that puts themselves and their own imagined existence after death above the people they love and who love them.

Teach them to avoid much of the best stuff life has to offer so they can stay on God's good side. Get them to accept privilege as their birthright, and how their privilege eclipses everybody else's rights. Teach them that society's laws are subordinate to God's laws. That God can supersede physics. That all theories are equally dubious. That evolution is a just a theory and God isn't. Teach 'em that no one is allowed to challenge their beliefs, and that any challenge is an attack. That they are born victims. Teach them to be hostile to science but to take advantage of its benefits. Teach them all about dinosaurs on Noah's ark and the rest of the literal-Bible, young-earth crap, and to avoid museums of natural history. Most of all, impress on their young minds that they are innately evil and deserving of the most hideous and unending torture.

Well, that is exactly what my folks taught me, and what Uncle John Wesley and Aunt Winnie taught Palmer, when we were little. Careful, though, this shit can go seriously awry on your ass. That's what happened with Brother Sam's people. You risk having your child wake up one day and realize that everything his people claim to base their values, their entire belief system, and their behaviors on, is a tissue of falsehoods. Unintended consequences are a motherfucker.

Speaking of unintended consequences, reading *Huckleberry Finn* wrecked my life beyond repair when I was ten years old, which I certainly did not intend when I took it up after Palmer turned me on to it. There was this other book we were trying to get through at the same time, the King James Version of the Bible, and it was horrible, only Palmer wouldn't admit that it sucked. Goddamn. *Huckleberry Finn* was way better, not only as a work of fiction, but especially as a moral guide.

What got me was that Huck was a boy about our age. The damage to my peaceable existence occurred when I got to Chapter Thirty One. Huck's conscience has been bothering him for not turning in his friend Jim to his so-called rightful owner. Up to that point Huck didn't know any better than to subscribe to the values, and follow the example, of the ones he was raised around. That's why he used such awful racist language as a boy; he learned it from all the upright church-going folks in his life. I was the same way till I outgrew that and God and the whole mess.

Anyway, Huck agonizes until he finally breaks down and writes a letter informing the authorities where Jim can be apprehended. Right away he feels good and all washed clean of sin for the first time, worthy, even, to pray, which he hasn't before. But he doesn't pray. He lays the paper down and sits there thinking —thinking how good it was it all happened so, and how near he come to being lost and going to hell. Then he gets to pondering how Jim told him he was the best friend he ever had in the world, and how much he loved Jim, too.

And this is where Huck ruined Jesus for little Brother Sam. Huck says, "I happened to look around and see that paper." He's referring to the letter ratting out Jim. Huck says, he says, "It was a close place. I took it up, and held it in my hand. I was a-trembling, because I'd got to decide, forever, betwixt two things, and I knowed it. I studied a minute, sort of holding my breath, then says to myself: 'All right then, I'll go to hell.' — and tore it up."

He tore it up. For Huckleberry Finn so loved Jim the Slave that he gave his everlasting life, he commended his own soul to hell, rather than betray his friend. Put Jesus in that position and see where you come out.

Jesus knew all along that sweet heaven was right there waiting for him just as soon as he got through that one crappy Easter weekend. Him pretending to die was just so everybody would say how great and selfless he was. Shame on Jesus. Praise Huckleberry. Everybody. Goddamn.

I realized that the believers around me would always put their made-up everlasting life ahead of my real life. It was always gonna be them first, God second, and little Brother Sam somewhere down the line, since whatever I could offer stopped way short of everlasting life.

And I have Huckleberry Finn to thank for that realization. God was already on probation by then, this just about put him away permanently.

It didn't do much for family relations, either; I can tell you that. Of course, so far as anybody can say, no actual Jesus ever existed. It appears he's exactly as real as Huck. Just not as noble.

All but the farthest flung extra-galactic Christians concede that much of the Bible is symbolic. Well, Jesus bullshitting folks about the nature and degree of his supposed sacrifice is the perfect metaphor for the ultimate selfishness of religion, the innate corruptness of the reward system, the black lie that coercion under pain of punishment is equivalent to a choice freely made. I'd say that the Bible got the symbolism about right.

Well, I'd take hell with Huckleberry Finn over heaven with Jesus Christ any day. Naturally, I was relieved to discover that there was no hell, and no Jesus to send me there. But I was somewhat disappointed, too. I was kind of looking forward to spending eternity in hell with, if not Huckleberry Finn, certainly Mark Twain. Naturally, Palmer saw Huck Finn as nothing other than an adventure story.

Both the *Adventures of Huckleberry Finn* and the Bible touch on the subject of slavery. The *Adventures of Huckleberry Finn* is against it. The Bible is for it. Believers live for the day they die and move onto the great plantation in the sky, where they can spend eternity heaping gratitude on the master— upon whom they are wholly dependent.

Well, Palmer takes the Bible at its word.

Palmer has faith. Faith. I am willing to accept, on faith, without one particle of evidence, that Palmer is educable. As much faith as I do not have in God, that's how much faith I do have in Palmer, if only because he hasn't disowned me like the rest of my people have. It is a bitter thing to know somebody you love considers you unworthy of being loved in return. It's something like being an atheist in the USA. You can be as patriotic and civic minded as an entire troop of boy scouts, but your country shows you the back of its hand.

Palmer thinks the government is at the heart of a great atheistic conspiracy. He hates the government. And has no regard for the rights of anybody who does not share his religion. Yet he's counted as more fully American than you and I.

An atheist group in Tulsa put up some billboards a couple of years ago, right where Palmer couldn't avoid 'em. And every time he saw one it made him mad all over again. So he waited 'til he was fit to bust, near about to soil himself with indignation, then called me. Palmer said, he said, "If atheists don't believe in God, then why do they have to call attention to that?" He said, "Atheists don't believe in anything! Free speech is for what you believe in, not what you don't believe in."

Can you believe that shit? I explained to Palmer how that is the same strain of willful cluelessness on the part of the believing majority that makes life as an atheist in the USA so fucking aggravating.

I know what those brave Tulsa atheists had to go through to put up those billboards. Same with other groups in other towns. Everyplace is the same. The few outdoor advertising companies who'll accept their trade require them to post bonds against damage by vandals, a condition not imposed on other customers. And wherever those billboards go up, the local believers respond with vandalism, threats, boycotts, and hateful harangues in the press. Desecrating expressions of faith counts as a hate crime. Vandalizing an atheist billboard doesn't. Which itself testifies to the fact that atheists are hated. And you know that's no idle claim. That is not whining about some imaginary or even historical persecution. Poll after poll, over many years, affirm that Americans despise atheists more than pretty much any other group save outright criminals, and even then it depends on the offense.

And just because so many believers express hatred toward Brother Sam, doesn't mean I have to hate them back. Somebody has to exercise some moral judgment. As I say, hatred, or even hostility, toward the misguided majority who believe in God is wrong. And dangerous. Brother Sam knows better than to throw down with the godly. Like I told Palmer, y'all godly are some scary motherfuckers. So I'll reserve my hostility for every form of tyranny over the mind of man.

Count the number of steeples and crosses and assorted pieces of iconography in your local skyline. Anybody ask any atheist you ever heard of if they were OK being surrounded by a bunch of religious bric-a-brac looks like it's straight oughta K-Mart's lawn and garden department only fucking huge? That's some tacky shit. One of its functions is to remind believers that they're in charge. Another is to remind you and me to like or lump it. And that's pretty goddamn tacky, too. But nobody's saying that believers shouldn't be allowed to clutter up the view with all the spires and minarets and whatever else they require to shore up their faith. Atheists are the first ones to stick up for anybody's right of free expression, however boorish and tasteless. Just so long as we're not being made to pay for said expression, and it's not on public property. Believers, on the other hand, tend to be less willing to turn the other cheek, in First Amendment terms. Let an atheist hang so much as one measly little sign on a goddamn bus. See how the believing class reacts.

Travel to any area of the USA and hunt for a public radio station, down there near the bottom of the FM dial, and note how, even in places no NPR signal reaches, every available frequency is taken up by charlatans pitching crap to the credulous.

What you do on private property, no matter how tasteless and inconsiderate, is between you and your neighbors. Hell, you can make like the goons at Westboro Baptist and festoon your church with "God Hates Fags" banners so that all the neighborhood children can't avoid seeing them, and there isn't a damn thing anybody can do. Well, that's not exactly true, either. I might show up and exercise my own goddamn First Amendment rights.

You see, what offends believers isn't just what's said, it's who's saying it. Christians in the USA sincerely wish atheists were godly, not in the sense of being good, in the sense of being nonexistent. And in the absence of that, they wish not to be reminded that atheists exist. Their preferred means of achieving that condition would be called "prior restraint" if the government were trying to get away with it. Well, the Bill of Rights protects us from the government pulling that kind of shit, but it doesn't prohibit our godly neighbors from doing everything their sanctimony-addled psyches can contrive to deny us full participation in the communities our taxes help pay for. And to freely speak. And you can't have anything like a free society when the second largest religiously-defined population (that'd be nonbelievers) has to clear its communications with the largest (that'd be Christians). There are five times as many nonbelievers in the USA as Muslims and Jews combined. Can you imagine nonbelievers being accorded the deference that either of those groups enjoy? By the way, you don't hear about atheists defacing religious bill-boards. Or any other kind.

Christianity is a faith such as requires but-tressing on a monumental scale. Never mind all the competing churches in the USA, an ever increasing number of which are of colossal di-mensions, designed by those without scruples for those without taste. And billboards warn-ing, threatening, browbeating everybody who uses the roads, to accept Jesus, or else. Not to mention the giant prefab crosses along the In-terstate. Look like something a monster robot Christ would climb down from and destroy To-kyo. If there's one thing every atheist knows, it's that the Believing Class usually get their way by dint of being a huge-ass majority with no com-punction about shoving folks around.

I have been ruminating on a discussion— I wouldn't want to say argument, with Palmer re-cently about his constant whining that Christians are being unfairly treated here in the USA. He's terribly afflicted with this self-induced mental aberration, Imaginary Memory of Ancient Per-secution Syndrome, IMAPS. And can't nobody out-snivel Palmer. He's already got that voice, sounds like he's straining at stool all the time; and you run that through a telephone receiver and it's about the pitifulest thing you ever heard.

So Palmer starts in on me in this voice, laying on the aggrieved party bit pretty damned thick, about how the Pentecostals in Burkina Faso or some damn place are being picked on by the authorities and he works it around in his mind that he and the slobbering glossolaliacs down to the Blood of the Lamb Pentecostal Assembly and Full Gospel Family Worship Center own a piece of that, that that somehow extrapolates into the oppression of Christians everywhere in general, and in the USA in particular. And it's atheists like Brother Sam have to answer for it. And watch our goddamn language when addressing or referring to the tragically oppressed Jesusites. Palmer and his pals don't draw any distinction between the junta in Burkina Faso water-boarding the indigenous holy rollers, and an atheist in Santa Cruz or Springfield simply and civilly speaking her or his mind. Torturing tongues-speakers and talking truth are equally odious to Palmer's Christian sensibilities. For him, Brother Sam stands in for everybody living or dead who ever declined to play along with the whole God game. With Palmer and his cohorts it's, "You're either for us or shut up." Did somebody say goddamn?

Better than eight out of ten Americans call themselves Christians, so when they cast themselves as some small sorrowfully put-upon fraction of the population, it looks a little shabby. That they're persecuted or oppressed is a threadbare old fib that's been told and retold so much that nobody any longer even questions its truthfulness, which, it turns out, is nonexistent. Like God. God's Truth. It is not only unseemly, but disingenuous for the privileged to comport themselves as victims, even if at some point more than one-thousand- seven-hundred years ago, in a land far, far away, somebody was persecuted for professing belief in an imaginary friend whose general description calls to mind the omnipotent play pal favored by twenty-first century Americans.

Better than eighty percent of my neighbors, most of my friends, and ninety percent of my family, are still making out like the situation for Christians hasn't changed since Nero was using them as yard lights.

The fact is, once the Emperor Constantine got right with the Lord, back in the year 313, the sandal was on the other foot. And Item A on the agenda, as soon as Christians took charge, was putting that foot up the ass of every non-Christian. And they haven't let up yet. Foot's still right up in that heathen ass. Complain about the foot and they accuse you of picking on them. Goddamn.

And they're still throwing their collective weight around, fiercely suppressing so much as a billboard or bus sign from the non-Christian minority, while moaning about how badly they, the majority, are treated. The last time Christians were persecuted in the USA was never, unless you count that dished out by other Christians: Quakers and Puritans and Catholics having to go off and start new colonies because they hated each other as only the godly can hate. You can't blame atheists for persecution served up by your spiritual kin. I can understand Christians being loathe to quit on something that forms so important a part of their identity. And I can tell what a charge Palmer gets out of thinking of himself in the same class as Peter and Paul and the saints that, in the years preceding 313 CE, got hanged or stoned or burned at the stake or renditioned to Babylonia. Nobody wants to get into matching victimhood with Christians. I mean, getting shoved around is nothing to brag about. But at least our victimization is up to date, ongoing and actual, unlike made-up memories of lions and crosses and fires and an ancient empire where, for awhile, Christians were a minority. Before they took over the fucking world.

And even though the assorted sects that make up the Believing Class have been acting in bad faith since long before there was such a thing as a USA, and show no signs of suddenly acquiring any regard for those other than themselves, even though they've rigged the system to work in their favor, and will swiftly and terribly slap down any opposition, some atheists would rather endure an endless succession of slights and injuries than risk offending those dishing them out. God forbid that a minority against whom the entire edifice of American culture is arrayed should, in challenging 400 years of theistic hegemony, employ language other than that approved by the Believing Class themselves. The many have always wanted docility and deference from the few. But atheists are starting to pay attention. Goddamn?

And anybody paying the least bit of attention has got to be miffed. Even, dare I say, angry. Anger is the only appropriate response to some shit. Anger, not violence, hatred, or even hostility. Just plain old anger can be a powerful motivator, a stiffener of backbones. And we need more of that. What we atheists have been doing up until now hasn't worked out so well.

In fact, after centuries of civil discourse, we're still subsidizing with our taxes the promulgation of what we oppose on grounds intellectual, ethical, and humane. Behaving ourselves has got us living in a world designed and decorated by people who don't give a shit about what we think.

And the first suggestion of anger or mockery or anything other than silent assent from the underclass sends believers into paroxysms of self pity, gets them crying to the high heavens that any affront to that privilege they regard as their birthright constitutes a grievous injury both unfair and indecent. In less time than it takes to form a thought they go from lords of all they survey to whimpering victims, whining that we few atheists are throwing them, the many believers, to the goddamn lions. Here's my proposition: fix it so that our government no longer uses my taxes to advance your predilections at the expense of my rights and get back to me on victimhood. Goddamn.

Palmer says that Brother Sam's show, Patriarchs and Penises, is purposefully offensive to believers. He has not seen it, of course. Palmer is very careful to avoid exposure to anything that might cause him to think, perchance to question or doubt.

A lot of folks, even some atheists, find it hard to accept that believers simply do not enter into to the process whereby a Sam Singleton, Atheist Evangelist show comes into existence. At no point do I pause and take into account the feelings of some unknown believer who may someday wander into one of my shows. I never attend church. And I do not argue the existence of God, or otherwise bandy words with church-goers, with the sole exception of Palmer.

When believers choose to join me and my atheist friends in a place reserved for our own free expression, they risk exposure to that which violates the sense of privilege they accept as their due in the wider world. They're welcome to come on in, but the privilege has to wait outside.

Another thing folks risk exposure to is adult language. I have been known to lightly season my speech with profanity, and not just goddamn with a little g, either. All manner of oaths and epithets. You can't beat cussing for getting folks' attention. And plenty of cusswords have no precise or concise synonym. I cannot guarantee that some folks will not be offended by my verbiage. But my aim is not to give offense, it is to communicate clearly. To amuse the bright and confuse the dim. I mean, goddamn.

Of course, were I to tailor what I say to suit Palmer and the rest of the Believing Class, I'd be a theist evangelist. And much, much more prosperous. Even so, on a number of occasions, admitted believers have expressed friendly surprise at having found the show more thought provoking than offensive. Not Palmer. I'm pleased when believers like the show. But that they do is incidental. They are, in effect, eavesdropping.

Excuse me while I wax nostalgic. When Palmer and I were boys, in Texas County, Missouri, those who could afford a telephone had to settle for a party line. Now, there wasn't any way to stop folks from listening in on their neighbors' conversations. But those who did ran the risk of hearing more than they wanted to hear. And learning how other folks regard you can be flat uncomfortable. If you're a believer, and you elect to come to a Sam Singleton, Atheist Evangelist show, you will absolutely witness what happens when the marginalized minority gathers to speak freely about the marginalizing majority. Expect to hear belief in God regarded with irreverence unto mockery, as surely as you will hear atheism decried in any of the more than three hundred thousand churches in the USA. Why, even now, believers are saying stuff that is repugnant to atheists. Some of them might even be saying mean things about me personally. Holding my values up to ridicule. Mocking my appearance and way of speaking, and otherwise expressing things that would make me uncomfortable, or even angry, were I within earshot. Well, I never was one to listen in on the party line. My advice to the Believing Class is to follow Brother Sam's example. And remember that I do not set out to make you mad. That's just a happy accident. Goddamn.

The low down mendacity that Brother Sam's anger does injury to the cause of atheists' rights is one that I take particularly vociferous exception to. You gotta expect believers to be looking to pounce on every utterance of the kindliest and, yes, most respectful, atheist evangelist ever to come down the pike; but fellow atheists? Goddamn. Some of us have apparently been infected with the same ovine identity germ that causes believers to mistake themselves for sheep.

Out here on the sawdust trail, an atheist evangelist hears certain phrases more often than others. A couple of years ago everybody was comparing atheists to cats, or the organizing of atheists to the herding of cats, a simile I first heard applied to first-graders. Fortunately, it seems to have about run its course. But atheists, insofar as I have observed, do indeed resist herding. And we may bear other similarities to cats besides independence of will. And I'm not just talking about cleaning ourselves regularly, or being capable of learning where it's permissible to piss and shit. For one thing, atheists are smarter than sheep, or at least smart enough not to go around bragging about how much we resemble sheep. You never see a cat trying to pass itself off as a sheep. The cat says, "I am a cat. You want somebody to boss around, go find you a sheep."

Sheep as role models offer certain advantages over cows, the other main herd animal. You get the most efficient use out of a sheep while it's alive. Whereas cattle, with the exception of milk cows, achieve optimal utility only when you kill 'em. Not only do you not have to slay a sheep to shear it, but, except for a few far-flung places such as Mongolia and Kentucky, mutton is scarcely regarded as food fit for human consumption. And any possum can tell you that tasting like shit is an excellent evolutionary strategy. Most places. But lamb is delicious. Everywhere. Deliciousness is not the main thing you want to have going for you. (Ask any pig.) All a lamb has to do is age out of its succulent lamb-hood and it has an excellent chance of spending the remainder of its days decorating some pastoral tableau unmolested, save the occasional shearing. Until its eventual betrayal and horrible death.

My uncle John Wesley, that's Palmer's daddy, worked at a slaughterhouse. He told how they kept this goat, the Judas goat, around for the express purpose of literally leading stupid, gullible, trusting, adorable little lambs, and tired old sheep, to the slaughter. "Follow the goat," says the sheep. "He looks like he knows where he's going." All the goat cares about is his own self interest. The goat sees one snack for itself as worthy of the lives of a whole flock of sheep. "Fuck 'em," says the goat. "Stupid sheep. Give me my carrot."

So, from an early age I knew to look out for goats. But I couldn't always tell for sure who was a sheep and who was a goat. Then I realized that it is not enough to know your goats from your sheep. You cannot trust a sheep to do any more than blithely follow the other sheep, who are following the goat. "If the blind lead the blind, both fall in the ditch": Matthew 15:14.

Blind trust, faith, eagerness to follow stupidly along, is how tasty little lambs get transsubstantiated into chops and cutlets before their first haircut, and how old ewes and rams, after a lifetime of fleecing, get rendered into grisly, rank mutton.

"All fall in behind Reverend Billy G. Gruff! Next stop, the cat food aisle!"

There are plenty of self-ordained leaders, and, call 'em what you will—pastors, preachers, popes, priests, imams, evangelists, grifters, gurus, governors of Texas, goats: they make their living betraying those who trust them, delivering the oblivious unto oblivion. For pay. But the metaphor falls apart, you take it too far. Not even sheep give the goat their money. And you, as a person, can decide whether to follow the goat onto the moral and intellectual killing floor. And even then and there, you can rise up, rinse off the blood, tell the other sheep, the goat, and the guy who owns the goat, that you have ceased being a sheep. Hell, you may even join the cats.

As for me, feline or ovine, caprine, bovine, porcine, or marsupial, I'd as soon be spared comparisons to the rest of the animal kingdom. I got all I can do just being human. Likewise being likened to a first-grader. Too much to live up to.

Anyway, I cannot spare Palmer. And what's worse, in spite of what I said before, I do care what Palmer thinks. All the other believers on earth? Fuck 'em. But it bugs me that, over all these years, I have been unable to get Palmer to see that he is completely full of shit. Which he is. He's the only believer I will discuss God with, and that's just because I refuse to totally give up on him. And he won't give up on me, either. It puts the both of us in a fix, but we live with it. I look at Palmer and see wasted potential. I think of the fun he should've had, but allowed himself to be screwed out of on account of some silly ideas about invisible creatures and imaginary places and life after death. I cannot help but expect better of Palmer. If it's possible to feel regret on somebody else's behalf, I regret all the things, good and bad, that Palmer has missed. You've heard about how you've got only one life, and if you do it right, one is enough. Should I, in my final moments, feel a need to count my regrets, I hope that they include mainly things I've done, not things I've missed.

As sure as folks can learn to make like they're sheep or goats, they can learn not to. Most atheists used to be believers. I know people who spent forty years pretending to be God's livestock and quit. And it could happen with Palmer, too. He is smart enough, and decent enough. Plus, unlike when I wised up at the age of fourteen, Palmer has somebody outside that hole who believes in him, his faithful cousin, Brother Sam. Goddamn.

Patriarchs and Penises™
A Comedy in Two Acts

Act II

Has everybody got their Sunday School Quarterlies? As you can see, this week's lesson is entitled *Patriarchs and Penises*. Now, I'm not usually a man to just go and talk about penises. But that's the lesson. As for Brother Sam, since I came of age I've learned that there are times when it's not appropriate to talk about penises. This is not one of them. But I am limiting this discussion to ancient penises, except when I talk about God's penis, which, of course, does not exist. Or is the same yesterday, today, and forever, depending on how your medication is holding out. And the only way to think about God's penis is in terms of the penises we know. Fortunately we were made in his image, so we have that to go by. If we look like God, God must look like us. Penises, too.

I'd been hearing about the bible my entire life, and had read a fair amount of it, but it wasn't until I was 14 that I decided to plow through the whole damned thing and see for myself what was in there. What I found was mainly about penises. Nobody had ever explained to me that what tied the whole book together, it's narrative thread, was penises. Imagine my delight. For boys of a certain age, the innumerable synonyms for penis comprise the bedrock vocabulary of the mother tongue. Penis jokes, penis legends, are the proverbs and parables of puberty. Suddenly I saw the Bible as the sort of material that might go over big in the ninth grade locker room at Orval Faubus High. Circumcision jokes and a room full of naked fourteen year-old boys? I was Don Rickles at the Tropicana. You might say that the seeds of my ministry were sown right there.

So I'm explaining to the fellas how God creates man's penis in his own penis's image, or at least in the image he wishes he had, hoodie and all, then ups and decides he wants the foreskins chopped off.

"You know," God says, "I never really spent much time examining my hypothetical penis before. And now that I look at it up close, I think it'd be somewhat prettier without that foreskin on there."

Now, God, being God, just commands his foreskin to depart and thus it is gone. And he could do that with humans, too. When you're God, it's never too late to change your mind. But that's not how God operates. He made people just so that he could do experiments on 'em. Simply making all those foreskins vanish would be out of the question. Better to see what sort of entertainment value could be gotten out of them. Besides, they make a charming collectable, as I'll get to here shortly.

The lesson's title references patriarchs and penises. The very first qualification for being a patriarch is having a penis. Without one you are a matriarch. But having one is no guarantee. For all we know, Zeror could've been twice as massively endowed as Abraham and nobody ever started any religions around him.

The penis is the Patriarch's expressive medium. The great ones are still remembered for their creativity, boldness, and originality in its symbolic use.

Legend holds that the main Patriarchs are Abraham, his boy Isaac, and Grandson Jacob. I throw in Noah and Moses and David. And since Brother Sam comes from a Christian background, Jesus and the Apostle Paul. They're what you might call the Patriarchs of those who roll and are also holy. You could say God is the Patriarch of the Patriarchs. Let's start by examining his penis, since God's sex underlies a whole bunch of important stuff, like why do we refer to this thing as "he," as if it just had to male. I'd prefer to have the least possible in common with this cosmic malignancy. Anyway, from what I can tell, most of the ones that do all the talking and writing about God, don't think he should have a penis. And that, I do not get. Ask anybody, what is it that makes a man a male? You know what they'll say. So what is it that makes God male?

I suspected that God had it out for everybody who had a penis. And everybody who didn't. He hated women even more than men. That's why he only got laid that one time. And she was still a virgin when he got done. From what I could tell from the pictures, Mary was no sex vixen, but you never know with Catholic girls.

I'm going to take a minute and jump back to the beginning. Not of the lesson, of the bible. God creates Adam and Eve and ten generations pass. To you and me, that's maybe two or three centuries. But these guys have somewhat longer life expectancies. Noah was over 500 years old when he fathered his three boys Japheth, Shem, and Ham. Boy I'm glad he named them that. Six hundred when God told him to build an ark. And after the flood (you know the tale, so I'll spare you), Noah lived on for another 350 years.

One time when he was in his late 600s or early 700s, you know, middle age, he'd gotten himself drunker'n a fiddler's bitch, and was sleeping it off in his tent. You see, Noah is given credit for inventing wine. And naturally becomes the first wino. One thing about Noah, he never could stand to be in any way encumbered once he got a load on, so he divested himself of his raiments and passed out in his tent. And he was lying there this one time when in walks his boy Ham. Well, that will not do. There's a long list of rules about seeing your kin naked, although it doesn't get formalized until Leviticus 18, and it spells out exactly whose nakidity you are not to gaze upon. And your pa is right in there. And we have Noah and Ham to thank for that. Except for them, we could all look at our daddies naked and couldn't God say nothing about it. So there's that.

Ham tells Shem and Japheth that the old man's in there with his dick hanging out, and they go into his tent to cover him up, but they turn their heads, not wishing to see their 736 year-old daddy in the nude.

He wakes up, and when he hears about Ham having gazed upon him lying there, putz open to the elements, runs Ham off. Banishes him outright and curses him and his offspring to live in slavery.

Ham goes off to populate Africa, and thus Egypt, and his seed spills across the sea to what later becomes Phoenicia. That would make him the patriarch of the Philistines. And that's as good a theory as any, since the Bible doesn't say where they came from. The Philistines gave Palestine its name. And we haven't heard the last of the Philistines.

But, way before the Philistines show up, the children of Ham have the effrontery to attempt to reach the heavens through engineering and cooperation, the fabled Tower of Babel. God couldn't have that, so he blew up their tower and scattered the people who had been getting along so well and confused their tongues so they could never again achieve great things as a society. Giving racism the biblical justification claimed by the tribe known as the Bigots was happy happenstance.

Noah's grandson nine times over, Abram, was an Iraqi guy, or at least he came from Mesopotamia. We pick up his story when he's 99 and the Lord has told him to go circumcise himself— and do it to all the other men and boys in the family compound, including Abram's slaves and his 13 year-old bastard son, Ishmael. In exchange for parting with his wrinkly old foreskin, God promises him a whole bunch of stuff, starting with an additional A and an H in his name, so thereafter to he gets to go as Abraham. And as if that weren't enough, God's gonna see to it that Abraham gets credit for starting a whole nation. And it's gonna be God's favorite. But Abraham will have to settle for knowing that his progeny will be doing the actual nation building. Oh, and God says he'll help Abraham knock up his 90 year-old wife, Sarai, who's also his half-sister. And she gets an H for her name, too, so she can be Sarah.

And Sarah has gotten way past the menopause without bearing Abraham a free-born male heir. You can't be patriarch of shit, let alone three of the world's major religions, without a free-born male heir. Ishmael won't do, since he is the issue of Abraham's dalliance with Sarah's house-slave, Hagar, who Sarah, very sportingly, arranged for the old fellow to pork so he could have some kind of boy, even a bastard boy.

Abraham circumcises himself. It's possible God's joking. He loves putting Abraham on. And this is exactly the sort of lowbrow humor God goes in for. But Abraham falls for it. And what's worse, he also agrees to implement a brand new tradition whereby every male born into this nation will be sexually mutilated even unto eternity. The actual mutilation is to be part of a ceremony, so everybody gets to watch. And the guy doing the mutilating has to suck the penis when he's done. That last bit was still biblical law when the Apostle Paul, who started Christianity, did Titus. But somewhere along the line Christians decided that it didn't apply to them.

So you could say that Abraham single-handedly started the whole circumcision craze. Like piercing or tattoos. Actual amputation.

Well, God pays off. Sarah comes down with pregnancy. I'd admire the fact that they were still going at it at that age were it not for them being siblings. Picture a 90 year old woman pregnant. And nursing. "Aw Ma, do I have to?" Somehow you know that boy is going to have difficulties.

And it is a boy. And Sarah and Abraham just dote on him. Name him Isaac. Means "to laugh." He's their pride and, you know . . .

Here's a little of the text: *"And Abraham*

was an hundred years old when his son Isaac was born unto him. And Sarah said, Who would have said unto Abraham that Sarah should have given children suck? For I have born him a son in his old age. And the child grew, and was weaned, and Abraham made a great feast the same day that Isaac was weaned."

They all talked like that back then. Like my cousin Palmer says, if the King James Bible was good enough for Abraham, it's good enough for me.

There's more.

And Isaac, sick unto death of giving suck to the bosoms of Sarah of the more than 90 years, as they were exceeding in pendulousness and hangeth low unto the ground, so Isaac too rejoiced greatly. And unto his old age the son of Abraham could not look upon the uncovered breast of whomsoever he lay with lest he lose his erection.

And bastard boy Ishmael is scarred for life in so many ways. If having your hundred year old dad come at your pubescent peter with a pruning implement and commencing to carve away wasn't traumatic enough, "Just hold still, son, I just about got 'er," the old fellow drops to his knees and goes to blowing you right there in front of God and everybody.

Abraham's true calling was to see how much he could fuck up his two (OK, one and a half) boys. Next to himself, and Abraham really loves himself, the one Abraham loves most is God. By a fucking mile. The best Isaac can ever hope for is third place, maybe fourth, depending on how hot Abraham still finds Sarah. Of course, Abraham has a girlfriend on the side, so there's her. And Ishmael, who's supposed to go on to be a Patriarch for the Moslems like Isaac is for the other Abrahamites. So Abraham prefers God.

God waits till Isaac is grown, then tells Abraham to murder him as a— gesture of subservience. And you'd think Isaac might've wondered who would worship a god so inflamed with ego as to just up and order a man to murder his own son. No. Isaac was cool with the whole thing. That's how fucked up all this shit had him. Breast feeding.

And Abraham don't give a shit. If God told him to jump off a bridge— And God never had a lick of taste or restraint. Bigger and bloodier is always better. So you can see where America gets it.

The theologically inclined might say that the whole reason God ordered Abraham to whack his son was to test whether he was prepared to give up what he loved most. No. You only have to ask if Abraham expected good things to come his way for doing it. And the answer is, what're you kidding?

Anyway, at the last minute, right when Abraham is about to gut his own child, an angel stops him, says God was just fucking around.

Just wanted to see how far Abraham would go.
So God let Abraham kill a ram which had got
its horns stuck in a nearby bush. The big drama
with the boy was one incredibly perverse practi-
cal joke. That's what happens when you're God
and you have too much time on your hands. You
create the universe in six days, then what? Fuck
with Abraham. He'll do anything.

Including running off to his girlfriend instead of going straight home to his ever loving
sister and spouse Sarah after he accepted God's
dare about killing Isaac. Once Abraham got to
being godly he just couldn't stop. And what's to
say God wouldn't get another wild hair up his
great ass (and yes, he had to have one, and lo
his ass was exceeding in its greatness), and have
Abraham go off and kill any damn body? Abraham really would do anything. He'd kill his son
and anybody else in an instant if he thought it'd
help him get in good with God. Fuck everybody
else. What worried me sick when I was a child
was whether my father would choose God over
little Sam. Abraham chose God over Isaac and
everybody applauded him for it.

God was hell-bent on somebody's son getting killed. If not Isaac, then his own boy. That's
probably what made him change his mind. "Hey,
wait a minute. Abraham! Hold up. I think it'd be
twice as much of a hoot if I sent my boy Jesus
here down to earth and had him killed."

And Jesus is saying, "Couldn't you just carve

on my dick instead?"

And his Holy Ghost part says, "Oh, we're gonna do that, too."

Later, Abraham arranged a marriage between Isaac and his first-cousin. Intermarrying was not only condoned in this family, but mandatory. And no, being from the Ozarks does not make me some kind of expert on very small gene pools. But if you saw any of my female cousins you'd understand why the possibility of marriage to one of them was just as alarming as getting thrown over in favor of God.

Isaac's twin sons Jacob and Esau, who are also each other's second-cousins, can't get along. So Jacob goes off to live with his uncle Laban and winds up marrying his first cousin Leah and her little sister Rachel, which makes Laban his uncle once, and his father-in-law twice. Oh. And Jacob also takes Leah's and Rachel's slaves, Bilhah and Zilphah as his concubines. Between the four of his sexual partners he begets himself a dozen boys— and a girl.

God is big on changing people's names. Just among our little cast of characters, he does it to Abraham and Sarah and their grandson Jacob. Later on, we'll get to the Apostle Paul.

Most of the name changes are just God dicking around. Just God being God. But Jacob's was important because, well just listen. This starts out in the 34th Chapter of Genesis which goes: "*Jacob journeyed to Succoth, and built him*

*an house, and made booths for his cattle: there-
fore the name of the place is called Succoth."*

I know.

So this one time he's wandering around out
on the edge of Succoth just after dark, when this
total stranger comes up on him and wants to
rassle. So they grapple with one another all night
long till Jacob makes the crazy man say uncle-
in-law. And the crazy man turns out to be God in
the form of an angel, and offers to start referring
to Jacob as Israel if he'll let go of his leg. And
the famous twelve tribes come from Israel's, or
Jacob's, sons, who the fellas in first-hour gym all
agreed were the fucking evil geniuses of all time.
And they meant that in a good way.

Here's the story: Israel's one daughter, Dinah, gets defiled by Prince Shechem of Succoth
who, subsequent to the defilement, desireth to
make Dinah his wife. Spoiled little shit that he
is, Shechem goes whining to his daddy Hamor.
So the old man takes the boy to see Israel and
suggests a reciprocal deal whereby everybody is
free to marry everybody's sisters. And Shechem
offers Israel and the boys any dowry they can
name. Yes, I know that the groom providing the
dowry seems all ass backward, but this is the Old
Testament.

So Dinah's brothers say, "You can keep your
dowry, and we'll forget all about you doing Dinah thatta way, but you gotta show us your penises. We could not possibly let our sister marry

anybody with a foreskin, or anybody that hangs out with anybody with a foreskin. We'll tell you what. You and the rest of the guys in Succoth all get yourselves circumcised, and we'll let you marry anybody you damn please. Dinah, too."

Well, Shechem and Hamor are only too happy to convene the First Annual (and as it turns out, the Last Annual) City of Succoth Penis Pare-a-Thon wherein every penis in town is rendered asunder. They were thinking, how bad can it be? But they failed to allow for inflammation. And in those days the rendering was wrought with a sharp stone. That's scriptural, which I'll get back to here in a minute. And if you think it smarts when they first chunk your penis with that rock, just wait about three days. Long enough for the swelling to involve the entire groinal region. And as the Succothites are laying around nursing their deflicted dicks, the sons of Israel are just biding their time.

The bible says, *"When it came to pass on the third day, when they* (that's the Succothites), *were sore, that two of Dinah's brethren, took each man his sword and came upon the city boldly and slew all the males. And they slew Hamor and Shechem his son with the edge of the sword, and took Dinah out of Shechem's house and went out."*

The sons of Israel came upon Succoth boldly! That's right. Waited 72 hours then came upon them boldly! "Whose ass you kicking now, motherfuckers?" And after they slew all the Succothites, they cleaned out the whole town and took all the women for themselves. Would've made their great-granddad Abraham proud. Unlike so many bible stories this one has a moral. Know who you're fucking with.

In spite of, or because of Abraham's selfless example, and the inspired deviousness of his great-grandsons, circumcision catches on. By the time Moses gets plucked from the bulrushes a half-dozen or so generations later, it was goddamn de rigueur. And when Moses grows up and gets married and the lord commands him to return to Egypt to tell Pharaoh to "*Let my people go,*" well, just listen, and see can you follow verses 24 through 26 of the fourth chapter of Exodus:

"*And it came to pass, by the way, in the inn, that the lord met him, and sought to kill him. Then Zipporah* (that's Mrs. Moses) *took a sharp stone* (a sharp stone)*, and cut off the foreskin of her son, and cast it at his feet, and said, Surely a bloody husband art thou to me. So he let him go. Then she said, A bloody husband thou art, because of the circumcision.*"

See? Bibledygook. Anybody who still maintains that the King James Version of the Bible is a divine example of top-notch prose, ought to have to write a book report explaining what the hell's going on in Exodus Four. No sooner does the lord give Moses a job to do than he tries to kill him without a word of explanation. And although the lord is the best there's ever been at killing folks, Moses survives. And as for the circumcision, I myself never could tell whether we're dealing with incest or spousal battery.

Either way, say what you will about the supposed hygienic benefits of circumcision, this isn't the fucking Stone Age. Since then we've learned about this infection control thing they got going.

Of course, Moses isn't famous just for his wife bobbing their baby's bishop, if that's who she did it to. Moses did some other stuff too. Just nothing of much note, penis wise.

The Philistines were uncut. They were fighting the Hebrews over Gaza close to 12 hundred years before Jesus, back when Ramesses III was about to have a fit trying to fill his daddy's sandals in Egypt. Like the Egyptians, the Philistines were technologically way out in front. They had a navy. They were the only ones who could smelt iron. That's why the book of First Samuel goes on and on about Goliath's armor. The Hebrews may have been stuck in the Stone Age because they were always having to pacify God instead of doing something useful. But they could still whip anybody with a foreskin, iron plating or no.

The Hebrews are saying to each other, "If this god whose name we're not supposed to mention would quit fucking with us for five minutes, we could build pyramids."

Pyramids? God hated the Egyptians. But he also hated the Persians, the Syrians, and the

Babylonians. Most of all he hated the Philistines. Goddamn Philistines. Not only did they get into it with the bible's protagonists, the aforementioned Hebrews, but they took to hanging shit on God, talking about what a bunch of no-foreskin-having monotheists he and his military were, saying some pretty awful things about their heritage. You know right off that some heathen blood is fixing to be spilt. And you never saw a spree the likes of when David and his boys tore into the Philistines.

You ever hear how David got himself betrothed to his first wife? David slays Goliath, right? So even though he's a commoner, he gets in tight with King Saul, who promises to let him marry his oldest girl. Saul says, *"Bring me the foreskins—"* You knew that foreskins would have to enter into it at some point. That's what gives a tale like this its biblical sweep. *"—the foreskins of one hundred Philistines."* Saul, who's a double-dealing sack of shit, is banking on the Philistines laying some slaying on David. But God rigs the fight in David's favor. He hates Philistines in rough proportion to how much he loves foreskins. He loves them so much that he's just naturally supportive of any activity in which they figure. So God helps David bring Saul not one hundred of the little morsels, but two hundred. Well yeah.

We can assume that David and his crew slew the Philistines before performing the procedures, but who knows? Maybe they just forced them to stand real still with their tunics h'isted up for as long as it took. They must've left the rest of the genitals intact, since it says nothing about lobbing off anybody's penis or nuts, which is not the kind of detail the Bible would omit. The only reasonable conclusion is that the Davite infantry slew the two hundred Philistines, then stayed around and individually altered their peckers. All 200 of 'em. "Holy goddamn! Seems like we've been at this for a week! And I thought peeling potatoes was bad."

And they did not offer the Philistines a chance to convert, either. If they had, and were called upon to get into according-to-hoyle, ceremonial circumcisions, they'd've had to have done the sacred sucking of the penises. That alone would've taken all day and half the night. And you know Philistines and blow jobs. They're gonna invite the Hebrews to stay over.

King Saul's shenanigans get him on God's short shit list and he ends up killing himself. And guess who becomes king?

For Christians, David is important because he's at the heart of the shaggy dog story that kicks off the New Testament. You suffer through this endless litany of begats between David and Joseph before you realize that if Mary was a virgin, and Jesus was sired by the Holy Ghost, Joseph's ancestry had nothing to do with anything. He was just some guy with a donkey. He was not

Jesus's biological father. If you tested Jesus's DNA for heredity from David, the results would be negative. They were not kin. And if anybody in Jesus's family was in line for the throne of Judah, like the Messiah was supposed to be, it was Jesus's little half-brother James, otherwise known as the Beaver. Everybody knew who his daddy was.

Jesus, being part of the godhead and all, must have been right there with his pa and the Holy Ghost when the order came down from himself about the circumcision. You gotta wonder if he said anything to the other godhead units. You know, "Let this cup pass from the third of us that's me?" I tell you what, it's the kind of thing a boy's likely to hold against the old man. But you can't argue— All the time that elapsed between Isaac and Jesus? Several centuries? That's how long it took for God and the Holy Ghost to pry the Son's grip loose. You can still see the claw marks on the pearly gates.

This was the run-up to the first Christmas. And I refuse to talk about Christmas. Except that, as the Gospel According to Luke says, "*And when eight days were accomplished for the circumcising of the child, his name was called Jesus, which was so named of the angel before he was conceived in the womb.*"

Doesn't say which angel. I'm thinking the Angel of the Highly Unlikely. Or the Angel of You Better Think Up Something to Tell Your Daddy.

What if the guy's knife had slipped and wrecked the little savior's schlong? "Oh never mind. I wasn't planning on using it anyway." And now eight different catholic churches in Europe claim to have Jesus's foreskin.

Now, about that "conceived in the womb" part. You heard correctly. Listen to that and tell me that God does not need to see somebody. This old boy can't even think of a penis without wanting to take a knife to it, and is so terrified of a vagina that he has to rely on artificial insemination to get his son conceived. Come to think of it, that means every egg implantation and every in-vitro fertilization is an immaculate conception. We're raising up a generation of blessed redeemers.

It was fifty years after Jesus died that the Apostle Paul invented Christianity and evangelism and ordained himself bringer of the good news to the Greeks and the Romans. Other than that, everybody probably would've forgotten about Jesus. The gentiles were all walking around with intact penises. All these guys get to middle age, but as soon as any of them got saved it was, "Hats off, fellas! Break out the blades, men, and let's get at them ding dongs." Timothy, always a good sport, got himself cut as a grown man. Now that takes a properly committed Christian. Titus let Paul circumcise him. And we won't even go into all the time they spent washing each other's feet. There're guys in San Francisco pay good money for that.

If the world was any less crazy, this shit wouldn't have caught on and couldn't have spread. But it did, all over hell and back again. So now the followers of the Patriarchs are Legion for they are many. As I said in the beginning, world-wide, the Abrahamically unaffiliated constitute a minority. If anybody's oppressing the godly, it ain't us. On the goddamn contrary.

Looks like my time's up. Next week's lesson is entitled "Messiahs and Major Muscle Groups." So be sure and study your quarterlies. This has a been a time of blessed fellowship for me. And I hope you've found it edifying.

Epilogue

Some of y'all know what it is to have endured endless hours of a church service, and think you're home free, only to have the preacher feel led of the Lord to convene an altar call. It goes something along the lines of, "I'm going to ask everybody to close their eyes. That's right. Now, with every head bowed and every eye closed, is there anybody here who is not absolutely certain beyond any shadow of a doubt that if Jesus called you tonight that you'd be ready?" Now, this could be prolonged indefinitely. All the while you gotta sit there without a fucking twitch. It's enough to put you off God for good. It did me.

In fact, if you have ever been a believer, if you have ever been baptized, if you have ever been hauled to church against your will, I want you to raise your hand. Just slip it right up and put it down again. Nobody will see you. Is that everybody? I will not prevail on you to further signify. Y'all already been through enough. So everybody who did not raise their hand, I want to come forward. Yes. Don't worry about looking silly or feeling awkward. It's natural. Come on up.

Instead of a sacrament, I like to think of this which we are about to enact as a sacrilege. What I have here are rocks. And as I confer one on each of you, I want you to bend down and just slip it into your shoe. Work it down in there where it pokes at you. Put your weight on it. Now, limp on back to your seat and reflect on how you wouldn't want to go through life that way.

Psalms 78: *And they remembered that God was their rock.*

And y'all who declined to participate? Y'all some hard-core atheists. Won't have any part of belief, even in the metaphorical sense. Well, God bless you. In the ironic sense.

Now we arrive at the Benediction, an exercise in irony if ever there was one. 'Cause Brother Sam ain't blessing shit. A wise and handsome man once said, "Luck is a good description and a terrible explanation." Well, I count myself lucky to be here with y'all. I can't appear at a gathering of atheists without remarking on how special it is to be in the majority for awhile. It's stimulating. It feels good. It feels safe.

Epilogue

So, latch onto as much of what we're all feeling right now as you can, and pack it out of here with you. And nurture it, so that when you feel outnumbered, when it seems that everywhere you look you can't see anything but crosses and steeples, when all you hear from political leaders is backward bullshit, when otherwise decent people give themselves over to the illogical, immoral and uncivil pursuit of selfish superstition, so that in the face of all that, you can summon forth the power of this great multitude. Because we're with you.

Goddamn.

Why Brother Sam Is
not Brother John

My great grandfather, John Foxe Singleton, named my grandfather John Clark "Pap" Singleton, for the first Methodist minister in Missouri. Pap's brothers, John Broadus, John Bunyan, and John Gill, were likewise named for preachers. And if you find it odd that the patriarch of a tribe of Pentecostals should bear the name of a Methodist, permit me to note that even though speaking in tongues seems quaint and old-fashioned, it is a fairly modern phenomenon. There were no Pentecostals before the twentieth century. The contagion has been traced to outbreaks of babbling in Kansas and California at Holiness revivals in 1906 and 1910. And that strain of holiness came out of Methodism. Thus, holy rollers are the spawn of Methodists, although neither side does much bragging about it these days.

Just as his own father had done, Pap continued the famous-preachers-named-John theme with all his boys, beginning with my uncle John

Travis, after the second Methodist minister in Missouri, then continuing through John Wesley, John Fletcher, and John Calvin.

Pap was the only one anybody addressed or referred to as John.

I have many times been asked why my name is Sam and not John. Well, at the time of my birth my father was on the outs with Pap. By the time they patched things up, I had been named Sam out of spite, and because neither of my folks knew any Sams. Even though I always suspected that that prejudiced Pap against me, I grew to see my name as setting me apart—which I was all in favor of.

The fact was, by the time I, the only son of the youngest brother, was born, the rule about naming Singleton boys John was becoming more difficult to enforce. Pap had used up the last of the famous preachers named John, at least up to that time. When my uncles got around to naming their boys, they were down to sticking just any old preacher's surname in there between John and Singleton. Palmer's big brother, John Moody Singleton, got his middle name from D.L. Moody. Uncle John Fletcher's eldest, my cousin John S.W. Singleton, has as his full name, and I shit you not, John Smith Wigglesworth Singleton, from this old time English preacher. He goes by Smith. When we were children we called him Wiggles, which always made him mad. Still does.

I'm fine being Brother Sam.

Why Atheists Always Lose When
Debating the Existence of God

Many of the atheists Brother Sam admires have been going around debating all over the place; and not just with each other, which is to be expected, even desired, but with believers, too—actually debating the existence of God, as if that's at issue. In public. I shit you not. If you truly believe, as Brother Sam does, that the existence of God is just as preposterous as that of Santa Claus, why the hell would you deign to debate that? Anybody seriously claiming to base his values and morality on the belief in a literal Santa Clause lacks the standing to argue before reasonable people. Come to think of it, it doesn't matter if it's one person or three billion. And as far as the merits of the proposition go, it's irrelevant that most of the people in the world believe in God, including some who are presumably smart enough to know better. If there are a sufficient number of Santatarians, people who profess belief in a literal Santa Claus, we're gonna debate them, too? What're we all, in fucking kindergarten?

Debating believers is degrading, not only to you (whether or not you recognize it), but to atheism and to the tradition of debate itself. Puts me in mind of that tired old saw about never rasslin' with a pig; you wind up all wore out and covered in mud and shit, and the pig enjoys it.

To believers who might feel some disappointment at being forever precluded from mentally martyring themselves on the rapier that is the wit of Sam Singleton, Atheist Evangelist, I will offer only this: So long as you're the one making the claim, the burden of proof is on you. I ain't claiming shit. You can go ahead and state your case; hell, you might even find a professional atheist with a book on the bestseller list to rebut it. But not me. I don't have to prove that God doesn't exist. It's understood. And I'm not gonna argue with you about it. Unless there's money involved. Brother Sam may be highly principled, but he's also reasonably priced.

Brother Sam's Rules
of Engagement

You might reckon that anybody as aggravated with theists as Brother Sam is would just naturally be looking to argue with any of 'em anytime, anywhere. But no. As I've previously explained, when I decide my pearls need casting, I'll choose which swine to fling 'em at.

When I was younger, anybody started an argument, I'd get onto 'em like a rat terrier and not let loose till I'd detached 'em from their dignity. But I quit all that. At least when it comes to B's, which, as you'll recall, is what Brother Sam favors calling believers. Besides, the people who most like to argue are rarely any good at it, so it's no fun whipping up on 'em. Yappy little dogs. I pay 'em no mind so long as they don't hump my leg or make a mess on the floor.

It took me way too long to realize that I was not bound to argue with any old body just because they raised a point I took issue with. Over time I devised a little checklist that I've sort of internalized, and I just go down that list in my mind whenever it looks like maybe somebody thinks they want to take on Brother Sam. If I cannot answer yes to each of the questions, fuck 'em. There are, of course, exceptions, which I'll get to shortly. But the main thing is simply taking time to think about whether to get into it. You'd be surprised at how the number of tussles I found myself in decreased once I started pausing first. And don't get the idea that argument, or for that matter arguing, is bad—far from it, so long as it serves a purpose.

Alright, back to the list. I'm not saying that these points aren't obvious, just that they came to Brother Sam over time. These are my criteria, yours may be different. Maybe for you nine is too many or not enough.

I have previously explained why I do not debate with theists. Now I'm fixing to explain why I don't argue with 'em either. As the Gospel According to Merriam Webster puts it, "to contend or disagree in words."

The first thing I want to know before I go to contending with anybody is whether we can agree on the words we're arguing about. Our terminology. This is an absolute requirement. And the more straightforward a term seems, the likelier it is that somebody will have some totally erroneous idea of its definition, and that's what they want to argue.

If each person is allowed to go by his own definition, we're never gonna get anywhere. So we have to agree to defer to the same authority. That's **Number two**. When it comes to authorities on definitions, Brother Sam is big on dictionaries. Pick one of the top five and consult it. There's your goddamn definition. Everything else is horsehit. And just so you know, The Gospel according to Merriam Webster has only one definition for atheist and it couldn't be simpler. "One who believes that there is no deity."

Item **Number Three** on my list is, am I amenable to persuasion? If there's no real possibility that I'll change my position, forget about it. Don't waste your breath and my time. You're not going to bring me around to accepting that the earth is flat.

Likewise **Number Four**. I ask if my opponent is amenable to persuasion. The odds of me convincing a fundamentalist to acknowledge that God is a cruel joke played on trusting children are too low to fool with. Fuck 'em.

Which naturally brings us to **Number Five**, which is another stopper. Can we remain civil and respectful? I'm not talking about profanity. After all, I don't argue with children, so I am free to speak as an adult. The question is, can we control our emotions? Brother Sam does not countenance name-calling and will not be yelled at.

Number Six: Do I care what my opponent thinks? It is not always a stopper, but it ought to be. Why flatter somebody you don't give two shits about by indulging their belief that their opinion matters to you. Know when to say, Fuck 'em.

Number Seven: Do I know what I'm talking about? I've learned that, however tempting, and easy it is to get swept along in the tide of enthusiasm, that you don't try and fake knowledge, or worse, just start making up shit as you go along. Know what you know and avoid going beyond that. You get in the habit of bullshitting folks and one of these times you're gonna run across a bona fide expert in the very field you're carrying on about and he or she is gonna open up your ass like a can of beans for all the world to enjoy.

Number Eight asks the same of my opponent. Don't argue with anybody who might turn out to be an idiot. And that

right there eliminates pert near everybody except Brother Sam.

And finally, **Number Nine,** is this worth
my time; is it worth arguing about? And
though it's closely related to several other
points, this is the one that most often gets
overlooked until the argument is already
underway and you're no longer enjoying
yourself. Remember, you can say fuck it
at any time.

So there are my nine points. Like I say, the
main thing is recognizing that you're in charge
and to take a minute to reflect before wading in.

And there are additional considerations. For
one thing, if some bigmouth is spouting racial or
any other kind of hatred, and if by saying nothing I risk having others mistake my silence for
assent, I have a duty to speak up. And even that's
complicated by not wanting to dignify a remark
that is unworthy of a thoughtful reply. Which
comes back around to why I neither debate nor
argue with theists. The notion of God is unworthy.

The consideration to end all considerations
is, of course, getting paid. It gives otherwise
credible atheists leave to earnestly debate a
plainly frivolous proposition with the plainly delusional. Getting paid, though not an especially
dignified or noble reason to debate, is usually a
sufficient one. Of such lofty themes as dignity

and nobility, Brother Sam knoweth not of which he speaketh. And so he shutteth up. But I am all in favor of getting paid. I'll argue the existence of disembodied space psychiatrists with a panel of Scientologists, you pay me enough.

One last thing. Back to language. When I'm talking to somebody, whether it's an argument or debate or just a normal conversation, I never accede to having anybody jump on me for bad language. I am not talking about cussing at a ladies lunch or some shit. This is when I'm having a personal discussion with another grown-up. I don't use any words they haven't heard before. And calling somebody on their language is a chickenshit little power play that's really about imposing your rules on the other fella, and about putting him on the defensive. No. Me? If somebody says, "Watch your language," I take that as my exit cue. I'd rather go off and find an adult to argue with. The "Fuck you" on my way out is optional. I try to be sensitive to the situation.

One of the Lucky Ones

I know I go on and on about my holy roller up-bringing, but Brother Sam was one of the lucky ones. Once I got to an age, I could tell from all the speaking in tongues and folks getting slain in the spirit that my people were a bunch of nuts. But what if I'd been raised in a mainstream or even liberal denomination? Any idiot could see that the shit I was brought up on was wrong, but what if church hadn't been weird and scary and embarrassing? What if it was nice and warm and friendly? Maybe the kind of religion that you can settle into and sort of snuggle up with, is just that much harder to haul your ass out of. Like a comfortable old chair.

Try getting comfortable in the midst of a holy roller shit storm. Or just knowing that one could break out at any time. Keeps you on edge.

But maybe I was lucky that it was goddamn uncomfortable. The religion of my youth was like having a condom stretched over my entire head. That's exactly what it was like. It made everything look all distorted, and made it hard to understand what people were saying and what I was reading. I felt like I was suffocating all the time. My skull ached like it was being squeezed by a . . . condom.

All my sisters and cousins? Still got the rubbers on their heads. But again, I was lucky. Ninety percent of the time the condoms are effective at keeping out infectious agents like science and art. But if you can manage to start thinking for yourself, the condom gets all stretched out and porous and more and more stuff leaks through and eventually the whole thing dissolves, leaving only little red Ribbed-For-Her-Pleasure lines etched into your face. That's a small price to pay to breathe free.

Atheists at Prayer

Brother Sam has been meditating of late on what an atheist is supposed to do while other people are praying. And unless you're a hermit, or have no family or friends, it's damned near certain that one of these times you'll be sitting around a dinner table when somebody asks somebody to say grace.

And maybe you'd as soon postpone being written off as a total heathen until there's no turkey and dressing involved.

In such a situation as that, you're likely to find yourself momentarily suspended in that what-the-fuck-do-I-do-now? zone while you weigh whether it's less hellishly uncomfortable to stare straight ahead or to hang your head like a scolded child and risk your good manners being taken for having suddenly lost your mind. We'll call this Situation A.

Situation B is if you're at a wedding or a funeral. The last thing you want is to call attention to yourself or to appear disrespectful. As with A, it can be pretty damned hard to resist the impulse to at least look down if not to actually bow your head.

In both situations A and B, Brother Sam favors staring horizontally into the middle distance while thinking about beer.

C is where you're at some sort of mass observance like a graduation or convocation or some shit. That's your time to stand tall, or better yet, remain seated, with yours eyes wide open, proclaiming, "Why don't you people sit your godly asses down so we can get this shit over with and go home."

But back to A and B. There are alternatives to mindless compliance and outright defiance when faced with the pressure to pray.

You can look startled and say, "You're kidding, right?" Or just for fun start praying out loud at the top of your voice. Say anything you like, although painfully personal stuff is best. "And I bless you Jesus for touching that scaly patch on my scalp, and we just ask you to deliver Uncle Duane from the masturbation."

Or quietly bow your head like everybody else, but when the Amen is said, just keep sitting there with your head bowed and your eyes closed for as long as you can stand it or until somebody has to tell you to stop.

But when one of these moments arises, I'd guess that more than a few of you just go ahead and bow your heads. And once you've gone that far you might as well close your eyes, too. You're gonna act a fool, no point in half-stepping. You may intend it as a gesture of respect and courtesy, but it sure looks like praying. Excuse me if I don't join in. In Brother Sam's line, praying is bad for business.

Gimme an *A*

Can't nobody tell Brother Sam nothing about the abuse gets heaped on atheists every day. I'm a goddamned authority. I figure I get abused as much as about anybody short of Brother Richard Dawkins himself. But you don't have to be any full-time professional God slayer to feel the cold sting of stigma that comes with proclaiming yourself an atheist. There isn't a one of us that hasn't been talking to someone and, having divulged our atheism, gotten the look, the one that says You might as well just save your breath because I quit listening back when you dropped the A-bomb.

Even Brother Sam can see why so many atheists are casting about for a tag that isn't so off-putting to the believing class. As for me, I personally do not give two shits. The believing class can accept me as I am or kiss my atheistic ass.

But some atheists dislike the way the word itself defines us by our relationship to God. And that is a damn good point. But if you can't use atheist for that reason, you can't use non-believer or non-theist, either. After that, the euphemistic pickins go to getting slim.

I say, let's just call ourselves "*A's*" and have done with it. And yes, I understand that some people will accuse us being elitist. So let's all agree that the A just stands for atheist and not being at the front of the line. God forbid atheists should ever be at the front of the line.

Believers can be *B's*. It'll do 'em good.

We *A's* need a symbol. Can't nobody compete with the B's when it comes to symbols, so we'll have only one. And since plenty of atheists already use the Scarlet *A*, (Brother Dawkins's Come Out campaign is big on the Scarlet *A*) Brother Sam is prepared to throw his full support behind adopting it as our entire iconography, although we might want to consider changing the color to blue or green so the B's don't mistake us all for adulterers.

And speaking of Richard Dawkins, he thinks atheists should be called "Brights." The idea of referring to myself as a bright gives me the creeps. Whatever my secret notions of my own braininess, I would stop short of just coming right out and saying I was bright, even though the word itself was preceded by an indefinite article. If I was Richard Dawkins, maybe. But I say it, and I right off sound like a horse's ass. Anybody who goes to mixing personal pronouns with the word bright gets me thinking that they're not half as goddamn bright as they think they are.

But I have no problem with calling believers non-brights or not-brights. And what's wrong with dulls? Darks is out of the question for obvious reasons. And I'm not saying that the *B* need stand for Backward or Behind or Below or Boob or any other pejorative. Surely a simple dignified "B" is to be preferred to any of those.

More troublesome is what to call agnostics, "*A*" already being taken. Under Brother Dawkins's naming scheme, they could be Not-So-Brights or Sub-Brights or Less-Than-Fully-Brights, Demibrights, Semibrights, Hemibrights, or Brightitos. Dims.

And just so my agnostic sisters and brothers know, trying to affix an identifier to agnostics is not easy, especially when you eliminate all the letters of the alphabet. What I came up with is the schwa (ə), which as you know looks like an upside-down little "e" and is pronounced, and this the part that really embodies agnosticism, uh. See? You don't have to actually call yourselves Schwas. For y'all, nothing changes. Somebody mistakes you for an *A* or a *B*, you just look at 'em and say, "I'm an uh—"

And if you can't abide the schwa, which I think more than does you justice, you'll have to settle for *C*. Confused.

Postcards from Paul
an
Epistolary Poem

The Saints
General Delivery: Thessalonia
P__ and Silvanus, and Timotheus,
   unto the church of the Thessalonians in
God our Father and the Lord Jesus Christ:
Grace be unto you, and peace from God our Father
   and the Lord Jesus Christ.
Ah, Macedonia! A pattern is emerging;
    no sooner do I found a congregation than
      I am compelled to exit under cover of night.
Add Troas.
You think you've heard commandments? Pish!
I've been wandering in the wilderness
    between my ears. Which reminds me—
      comfort the feebleminded.
You know, praying without ceasing,
    rejoicing evermore?
I wouldn't be much of an apostle if I failed
    to exhort you to abstain from all appearance of evil.
Actual evil? You decide. Prove all things;
    hold fast that which is good:
Pluralitus non est ponenda, sine necessitate.
Greet each other with a holy kiss;
    no, seriously, I'm not kidding.
Kissy kissy in Christ Jesus's name.
I'm sticking to my prophesy per
    the second coming; moreover,
      I bet He'll return like a thief in the night.
Sneaky.

Sam Singleton, Atheist Evangelist

The Saints
General Delivery: Philippi
P__ and Timotheus the servants of Jesus
  Christ,
    to all the saints in Christ Jesus which are
      at Phillippi with the bishops and deacons.
Lydia, oh Lydia . . .
Where was I?
You should've seen the first draft—
  rife as it was with compound sentences.
I do go on.
All that sex talk in the past?
Let's leave it there.
I don't want to keep reminding you people,
  this is about the payoff of all time.
There's this thing,
  predestination,
    I believe I'll call it,
      and the only way you'll know
        you've got it is that if you do,
          you'll naturally comport yourself
            as befits one of the Elect.
Clue: those who behave well?
Maybe.
Romans?
As a rule,
  no.
The Jews?

Postcards from Paul

Here in stir,
   I've time to ponder the state of the church.
Your problem is one of consistency
   or the absence thereof.
We are all over the place.
Consolidation is what's called for,
   a common denominator.
I offer up myself as your example.
Do as I do.
Look how humble.
Salvation is solely for we who have,
   to the letter,
      concluded the very transaction
         the church in Rome still doesn't get.
Ask anyone,
   Judaism is a dead end.
True righteousness and the abiding
   joy that springs
      therefrom are obtainable only
       through Christ Jesus.
The thing with grace is its singularity,
   exclusivity,
      not so much who's in as who's out—
       those whom the Lord deigns spare
        on condition of eternal gratitude
        expressed through slavery
        and ceaseless fawning.
Obsequiousness unto holiness.

Sam Singleton, Atheist Evangelist

The Saints
General Delivery: Galatia
P__, an apostle, not of men, neither by man,
  but by Jesus Christ and God the Father,
    who raised him from the dead in Christ Jesus.
Twelve hundred years from now an enactor
  of fraudulent freedom will cite this very note:
Johannes Dei gracia, Rex Anglie, Dominus
  hybernie dux normmannie et auitanne.
But meanwhile,
  back in Macedonia (or is it Greece?),
    I declare, the churches I founded
      —I founded—
        shall have the right of free election.
No, they are most certainly not synagogues.
Where was convened your last meeting?
Some guy's shed. So stop saying it.
Again with the Jews.
I'm leaning ever more toward Dad's side
  of the family.
This idea of salvation by grace—
  I think it has legs,
    especially among indolent Gentiles
      for whom achieving everlasting glory
        without lifting a finger
          could provide sufficient incentive
            to come forward and be saved,
              Just as I am.

Postcards from Paul

The Saints
General Delivery: Corinth
P__, called to be an apostle of Jesus
   Christ through the will of God,
      and Sosthenes our brother.
I'm here in Epheseus.
Don't make me come up there.
Get thee onto the same page.
Someone from the house
   of Chloe ratted you out,
      passed me a note.
These abuses of conduct cannot stand.
The talk is of rivalries,
   of moral disorders.
While the Jews wait for a sign,
   and the Greeks seek wisdom,
      we are in for such rewards
         as you wouldn't believe.
I heard about the fornicating
   that's been going on.
      Stop it.
Your body is a temple.
I personally avoid all
   sexual contact and
      suggest that you do the same.
Flee from idolatry.
Men are better than women.

Sam Singleton, Atheist Evangelist

The Saints
General Delivery: Corinth
P___,an apostle of Jesus Christ by the will of God,
   and Timothy our brother,
      unto to the church of God
         which is at Corinth,
            with all the saints which are in all Achaia.
Let God be our comfort.
Timothy and I found trouble in Asia,
   barely escaped with our lives.
I heard from Titus
   that your church has been doing better,
      but that the Jews persist
         in claiming a higher authority.
The nerve of those people.
I'm abolishing the law of Moses.
I will be your father and you will
   be my sons and daughters.
I know my earlier correspondence
   made you unhappy. Parental prerogative.
Remember, I've met Christ Jesus,
   not metaphorically as you, but actually.
I have espoused you to one husband
   that I may present you as a virgin bride.
Jesus Christ is the type
   to check your sheets in the morning.

Postcards from Paul

pros 'Rômaious
General Delivery: Rome
P__, a servant of Jesus Christ,
   called to be an apostle,
      separated unto the gospel of God . . .
Jesus was —is—the manifest heir of David,
   his resurrection left—leaves—no doubt.
You can work it out.
As for me, keeping busy in Corinth. As for my Acts,
   ask Luke the physician and taker
      of dictation from Peter if with Silas I didn't
         one midnight pray an earthquake
            unto my captivity and rather than
               take it on the lam
                  when the prison walls tumbled,
                     stay to convert my jailers.
I remained until paroled,
   as befits one who walked with Christ Jesus.
No one believes me, but it's true.
When in the course of human events
   it becomes necessary for one people to take leave
      of their senses, let justification be
         their constitution.
And we know that all things work together
   for the good. I love God and have been called
      according to his purpose, off to Jerusalem.
Phoebe said she was heading your way.
If she wants to preach,
   tell her I said no.

Sam Singleton, Atheist Evangelist

Philemon
General Delivery: Colossae
P__, a prisoner of Jesus
  Christ,
    and Timothy our brother,
      unto Philemon our dearly beloved
      and fellow labourer.
I worry about Tychicus
  getting this mixed up
    with the rest of the mail.
Tell me you don't see some irony here:
  me still,
    as they say,
      under house arrest
        (arrest arrest is more like it),
          writing to ask you,
            faithful Philemon,
              to be kind to sweet Onesimus
(his very name suggests profitability),
  who having absconded himself
    to Rome,
      found me and was redeemed.
I've come to love Onesimus
  and would be glad to call him my own.
I imagine him doing for me here,
  and how much more tolerable
    confinement might be were his
    ministrations ongoing.
Did I mention how old I am?

Postcards from Paul

I am very old.
Old and feeble and receding and—
   well,
     old.
You must not feel pressured to give him over
   just because I'm old and but
     for me you'd be hell-bound.
I explained that he trespassed against
   his rightful owner by running away,
     and that Christ
       Jesus insists he give himself up,
        should you decide to exercise
         your rights of property—
          notwithstanding how old I am,
          and what a godsend
           a slave of my own would be—
           in which case,
            it would be up to you
           to reconcile:
            master and slave,
             brothers in Jesus Christ.
Mark, Luke, Demas,
   and the rest of the fellows send
     love and kisses.
Prepare the guest room.
If I don't die from old age in the meantime,
   one day I'll be sprung.
Then look out Colossae!

Sam Singleton, Atheist Evangelist

The Saints
General Delivery: Phrygia, Colossae
P__ an apostle of Jesus Christ, by the will of God,
  and Timotheus our brother.
To the church in Colossae, city of Phrygia,
  in Asia Minor,
    the same church started by Epaphras,
      a good friend of mine, and Archippus.
Home cooking.
Remember me to Philemon and Onesimus—
  master and slave, true,
    but their relationship is strictly scriptural.
Resist false teachings—
  anything from anyone other than me or my
delegates.
Be true to Christ Jesus, the head;
  the church is his body.
Is either headlessness or bodilessness less
  monstrous than the other?
We are thus all that stands between Jesus
  Christ and monstrosity.
Once one has died,
  is resurrection yet to be desired,
    whether whole or truncated?
Live as those who have risen with Christ Jesus,
  pierced high and low,
    but with heads and bodies
      intact and attached.
When you call me Saul I don't hear you.

Postcards from Paul

The Saints
General Delivery: Thessalonia
P__ and Silvanus, and Timotheus,
   unto the church of the Thessalonians
      in God our Father and the Lord Jesus Christ.
It's been, what, two months?
Say what you will of its climate, Therma,
   rebuilt as Thessalonia, City of Cassander's wife,
      is indeed favored by geography—
Bifurcated by the highway twixt
   here and points north of the Agean,
      blessed among the four divisions
         of Macedonia under Rome.
There, where Silas and I organized a church,
   beloved but stupid,
      you seem to have misconstrued
         what was told you about the advent.
The day of the Lord is at hand.
Choose your companions carefully,
   eschewing all who disagree.
Flaming fire,
   recompense for those who molest the lovers
      of Christ Jesus.
Return tribulation in kind with God's sanction.
Remember,
   those whom you slay are not your enemies,
      but your brothers.
Do not speak to me of redundancy.
My sanctity trumps your pedantry.

Sam Singleton, Atheist Evangelist

The Saints
General Delivery: Ephesia
P__ an apostle of Jesus Christ,
  by the will of God,
    to the saints in Christ
      Jesus which are at Ephesia,
        and to the faithful in Christ Jesus.
The Colossians are a handful.
We'll see.
Communing with my jailmates back here in
Rome,
  so many fond remembrances of carousing
    Ephesia's harbor,
      my own two years there,
        visiting the museum,
          fencing relics in the temple of Artemus,
            whose worship will surely see
          you all to hell,
           but for me.
God mentioned a scheme to offer
  redemption for the entire church.
I never know if he's joshing.

Postcards from Paul

Timothy
  General Delivery: Ephesia
P__, an apostle of Jesus Christ
  by the commandment of God, our Saviour,
    and Lord Jesus Christ, which is our hope.
My son in the faith, don't trade in fables.
The infidels here in Rome released me
  from prison.
Laws are made not for the righteous,
  but for the disobedient.
In you, I see me. My mother, too,
  was a Jew— my father a gentile.
My own mother and grandmother
  schooled me in the scriptures.
I'm reminded of your conversion,
  at Lystra, on my first visit.
And I want you know how much I admired
  your being circumcised as a grown man,
    what with the state of cutlery.
As soon as you're able to get around,
  I'm putting you in charge
    of the church at Ephesus.
Evangelize Phillippi with Luke and Salvanus.
Visit Berea.
May God reveal
  the divine design behind the infection.
Join me at Athens.
Bring unguent.

Sam Singleton, Atheist Evangelist

Timothy
  General Delivery: Ephesia
P___, an apostle of
  Jesus Christ by the will of God,
     according to the promise of life which is in
        Christ Jesus.
Why do I persist in the face of arrest?
The garum, of course.
Yes, and the circus.
And, without so saying, the baths,
  not to mention the oils.
Always the mission: conversion.
But always,
  the harlot of the seven breasts diverts.
I mean, these people are gentiles,
  and I a citizen, as much Roman as Jew,
     whose savior more resembles Hercules
        than Jehovah.
Yet again I'm up on charges. Enough.
Regards to Silas. No to the file.
My son in the Gospel,
  assume the pastoral mantel, take up the staff.
Do these things in my name
  and that of Christ Jesus.
By these presents you are an exhorter
  of the Good News.
Your place is here (Rome, not necessarily jail).

Postcards from Paul

Titus
  General Delivery: Crete
P___, a servant of God,
  and an apostle of Jesus Christ,
    according to the faith of God's elect,
      and the acknowledgement of the truth
        which is after godliness.
You were called of Christ Jesus to be an apostle.
Get to it.
How about when we were at Antioch?
  and Jerusalem?
We were to meet in Troas but instead
  met in Macedonia. Such times we had.
And when I sent you to Corinth
  with the second note?
You must pick up where I leave off.
Organize churches all over Crete.
Appoint elders. Establish qualifications
  for officials and members.
The God-damned nonsense-speaking Jews
  and their filthy logic corrupts
    whole families at a time.
They must be silenced.
Those who would treat you contemptuously,
  treat as the Spirit moves you.
Keep an eye out for Artemas and Tychicus.
Wintering in Nicopolis,
I'll expect you.

Sam Singleton, Atheist Evangelist

In Memoriam
P__, scion of Tarsus, son of Celicia,
  Talmudic student of Gamaliel,
    speaker of Greek and Latin,
      reader of Greek and Latin poets,
        citizen of Rome:
O Pharisee bon vivant,
O hat check boy at the stoning of Stephen,
O epiphanic evangelist,
O peripatetic preacher
  who retaineth his day job as tent maker,
O repeat offender,
Who is struck blind on the road to Damascus,
Who meets up with Jesus
  fifty years after the crucifixion,
Who causes Peter and James to exchange
  nods and winks,
We knew Christ Jesus. You're no Jesus Christ.
Whose holy ghostwriter-amanuenses
  begins thirteen epistles "Paul,"
Whose name means little one, bald-headed,
  misogynistic fisher of men,
    beheaded in the bosom of the Holy See,
      who says that Christianity
        isn't the invention
          of a disgruntled secretary who
            engineers his own immortality?
Acta est fabula, plaudites!